THIRTY DAYS TO SPIRITUAL POWER

Thirty Days to Spiritual Power
Insights from Joshua and Judges
Alan F. Johnson

TYNDALE
House Publishers, Inc.
Wheaton, Illinois
COVERDALE
House Publishers, Ltd.
London, England

LIBRARY OF CONGRESS
CATALOG CARD NUMBER 75-13634
ISBN 8423-7090-0, PAPER

COPYRIGHT © 1975
TYNDALE HOUSE PUBLISHERS, INC.
WHEATON, ILLINOIS   ALL RIGHTS RESERVED

FIRST PRINTING, JULY 1975
PRINTED IN THE UNITED STATES OF AMERICA

Contents

INTRODUCTION

PART ONE
JOSHUA: A LEADER LED

INTRODUCTION TO JOSHUA
OUTLINE OF JOSHUA

DAY	
1	General Joshua *1:1*
	Promise and Possession *1:3*
DAY	
2	Orders and Resources *1:6, 7, 9*
	The Grace of God in an Ancient Hittite City *2:1–24*
DAY	
3	D-Day for Palestine *3:1–17*
	Lest We Forget *4:1–24*
DAY	
4	Consecration *5:1–12*
	The Commander in Chief *5:13–15*
DAY	
5	The Walls of Jericho *6:1–27*
	The Defeat at Ai *7:1–26*
DAY	
6	The Victory at Ai *8:1–35*
	The Integrity of the Scriptures *8:32–35*
DAY	
7	Compromise with Gibeon *9:1–27*
	The Day the Sun Stood Still *10:1–14*
DAY	
8	The Northern Campaign *11:1–23*
	Extermination of the Canaanites *6:21; 8:26; 11:11*
DAY	
9	Distribution of the Land *13–24*
	Possessing our Possessions *13:1; 18:1–6; 21:43–45*
DAY	
10	Caleb's Testimony *14:6–14*
	The Cities of Refuge *20:1–9*
DAY	
11	The Altar "Ed" *22:10–34*
	Joshua's First Farewell Address *23:1–16*
DAY	
12	Joshua's Final Farewell *24:1–33*

PART TWO
JUDGES: FAITH'S TRIUMPH IN TIME OF DECLENSION

INTRODUCTION TO JUDGES
OUTLINE OF JUDGES

DAY	
13	A Period of Declension *21:25*
	The Judgment of God *1:1–36*

DAY 14	The Causes of Failure *2:1–23* The Sin Cycle and First Judge *3:7–11*
DAY 15	How Well Do You Remember? *3:12–30* Women in God's Service *4:1–7*
DAY 16	The Alloys of Faith *4:8–23* The Song of Deborah *5:1–31*
DAY 17	The Call and Commission of Gideon *6:11–24* Clothe Yourselves with Humility *6:15*
DAY 18	The Self That He Wills *Philippians 2:5–8* The Preparation of Gideon *6:25–34*
DAY 19	Gideon's Fleece *6:35–40* Gideon's Three Hundred *7:1–8*
DAY 20	Gideon's Strange Battle *7:9–23* The Last Days of Gideon *8:22–32*
DAY 21	Abimelech: The Bramble King *9:1–57* Jephthah's Victory: Binding the Strong Man *11:1–29*
DAY 22	Jephthah's Vow *11:30, 31, 34–40* Jephthah's Vengeance *12:1–6*
DAY 23	The Birth of Samson *13:1–25* Samson at Timnah *14:1–20*
DAY 24	Foxes and Firebrands *15:1–8* A Thousand with a Jawbone *15:9–20*
DAY 25	Samson and Delilah *16:4–20* Samson's Death *16:21–31*
DAY 26	Samson's Epitaph *Proverbs 6:26, 27; 16:32* Micah's Idol *17:1–13*
DAY 27	The Road to National Idolatry *18:1–31* Moral Chaos *19:1–30; Romans 1:21–25*
DAY 28	The New Morality *17:6; 18:1, 7; 19:1; 21:25* What Behavior Is Right? *Matthew 15:18–20; Romans 1:32; 2:12–15*
DAY 29	Civil Chaos *20:1–48* Civil Rights and Civil Disobedience *Romans 13:1–7; 1 Peter 2:13–17*
DAY 30	Healing the Scars *21:1–25* Power or Defeat? *John 16:21–24*

SOME FINAL THOUGHTS

Every age has its crises. Ours, I believe, are twofold: crisis of *leadership* and crisis of *faith.* Watergate and the unprecedented fall of Richard Nixon illustrate the first. The proliferation of books on facing death without faith in God (such as Stewart Alsop's best seller, *Stay of Execution*) is an example of the second. Could there be any relationship between the two? The Bible declares there is.

Hardly any literature deals more relevantly with leadership and faith than two Old Testament books, Joshua and Judges. In the unfolding drama of God's redemption of his ancient people Israel, no greater leader arose than the young man Joshua. What kind of a man was he in those revolutionary days? How old was he? What did he believe? How had he proved himself in former days? What were his strengths and weaknesses? How did he face them? What kind of leadership did he give to the nation? The book of Joshua answers these and many more important questions about leadership and faith.

Joshua and Judges take us through dark nights of corrupt leadership and national disloyalty. We see failure, discouragement, slavery, immorality, violence, and unimaginable perversion. We witness the people of God exchanging their covenant loyalty to Jehovah for the idols and ways of the world. Yet even in the darkest hours, light flashes forth. God raises up strong leaders of faith in the true and living God. No wonder the writer of the New Testament book of Hebrews in the familiar eleventh chapter calls to mind men and women from the pages of Joshua and Judges: Joshua, Rahab, Jephthah, Gideon, Barak, Deborah, and Samson.

Introduction

PART ONE

JOSHUA: A LEADER LED

INTRODUCTION TO JOSHUA

Joshua is a book about victory with minor scenes of failure, while Judges records the failure of faith, with an occasional oasis of encouragement in the resultant spiritual wasteland. From the way God dealt with lives then, we can learn lessons to enable us to avoid the snares which trapped them. We can build a solid faith-life into our twentieth-century lives.

Joshua shows how a man and a people who received a *promise* from God also discovered the *power* to possess the inheritance of God through their faith. As we follow this man of God from the early days when he led the people through the Jordan River to conquer Jericho, to the twilight years when he delivered his final exhortation to the nation at Shechem, we will walk the paths of real people. They struggled with God's will for their day as we must for ours.

In order to give the study coherence, it will help to have an outline of the book of Joshua before us.

OUTLINE OF JOSHUA

   I. Invasion of the Land (chapters 1–12)
      A. Preparation (1–5)
      B. Central campaign (6–8)
      C. Southern campaign (9, 10)
      D. Northern campaign (11, 12)
  II. Distribution of the Land (chapters 13–22)
      A. Distribution to the two and one-half tribes (13, 14)
      B. Distribution to the remaining nine and one-half tribes (15–19)
      C. Cities of refuge (20, 21)
 III. Final Scenes (22–24)
      A. Consecration of the eastern tribes (22)
      B. Consecration of the western tribes (23)
      C. Joshua's final speech (24)

A final word. Take your *Living Bible* in hand and read each section of Joshua before reading these comments. This book cannot substitute for the living Word of God. If it can help you see some small feature of the Word, it will have fulfilled the author's intention.

Joshua 1:1
General Joshua

Key thought: *Behind every great movement of God there is a prepared man.*

This act from God's unfolding drama of redemption receives its title from the man who was the chief actor. Since Moses' impetuousness had cancelled his chances to enter Canaan, the privilege fell to his younger associate Joshua. What a tremendous task! To lead the millions of Israel into the promised land and to conquer the formidable strongholds throughout the country requires a man of unusual gifts and preparation. Joshua first appeared in the biblical record as a young man some forty years before our present chapter (Ex. 17:13; 33:11). He was already distinguished as the commanding general of Israel's military forces as they engaged the first hostile nation after their exodus from Egypt. Joshua's experience in military leadership throughout the wilderness journeying would develop his natural ability to the measure necessary to lead the invasion of Palestine.

Military prowess was not the only quality Joshua exhibited. He was Moses' constant aide and minister (Moses' assistant—1:1; cf. Ex. 24:13–16). Learning to take orders and serve another is an indispensable prerequisite to leadership. Courage and faith in God's promises were seen in him as he and Caleb brought back a favorable report after spying out the land (Num. 13:30). Seeing the background of Joshua as a young man fully devoted to the Lord (Num. 32:12), filled with the Spirit of God (Deut. 34:9), gifted as a prophet (1 Kings 16:34), and endowed with ability and intelligence, we can appreciate that this is the man

Day 1

whom God chose and whom Moses had prayed for and appointed to be his successor (Num. 27:12ff.).

Let us not minimize preparatory years as wasted years. Young people must be encouraged to prepare themselves to the limit of their opportunity. Inevitably the torch must be passed. It is the wisdom and place of those in receding years to insure that their leadership is passed on to able and committed young men and women who shall lead the invasion for Christ into the world of today.

Joshua 1:3
Promise and Possession

Key thought: *Promise is not possession until aspiration has by faith become experiment.*

The promise was given to Joshua that every place that the sole of his foot would tread upon, "to you have I given it." The land was Israel's by divine decree but she had to believe God, go in, fight, and take it. Here is an important principle with God and his people. Through our faith in Christ, God has bequeathed an inestimable inheritance to us (Eph. 1:3, 11; 2:6), but our possession and enjoyment of this wealth are dependent upon our appropriation by faith day by day of God's promises. "Possession" (*lox*) is the key word of the book of Joshua. Faith appropriates while aspiration merely agrees and admires. We can always tell the difference between simply admiring God's promises and possessing them, by our action.

Harry Ironside, the notable Brethren Bible expositor, used to tell the story of a gentleman who received a piece of property through bequest. Several years later he decided to sell it and had a broker write up and post a description of the estate. As the owner read over the realtor's report of the beautiful location, spacious grounds, shady trees, and comfortable home, it dawned upon him that this place was much better than where he was presently living. So he moved out to enjoy his inherited estate. Like so many Christians, he knew he had something, but the details were vague and he had failed to move into the enjoyment of what he possessed.

Joshua had the promise. With eyes wholly toward the Lord, he set his feet moving to transform the promise into possession.

Joshua 1:6, 7, 9
Orders and Resources

Key thought: *God's resources of his Word and his presence are never inadequate for his tasks.*

Having thus prepared the man for the task, God now charges Joshua with his mission and alerts him to the resources and conditions for success. It will be no easy job to conquer and divide the land of Canaan. Joshua needed threefold encouragement to see him on to victory. Each resource was accompanied by the exhortation, "Be strong and brave" (vv. 6, 7, 9).

The divine *promise* is once again repeated in Joshua's ears. "You will be a successful leader of my people; and they shall conquer all the land I promised to their ancestors" (v. 6). All of God's name (reputation) was behind the promises made long ago to Abraham, Isaac, and Jacob concerning the land (cf. Gen. 15:7; 28:13). It has been said often (but believed less often) that it is better to have a promise from God than a sizable bank account under the world's most stable government. In order to be firm and courageous Joshua would need to consider the condition in the next exhortation.

The divine *precepts* of the law of Moses must be observed (v. 7) in the entire effort if God were to bless. Obedience to God's revealed Word would determine Joshua's success in this daring conquest. More specifically he is to "remind the people constantly about these laws" (v. 8), not by preaching, but rather by talking about God's Word and reading it aloud. But more than talking and reading, we are to practice thoughtful application of these truths into everyday living. Joshua was to talk of the truth, think of it, and

Day **2**

to do the Word. Such an approach would lead to blessings of success.

Finally, the divine *presence* is promised Joshua (v. 9). "The Lord your God is with you wherever you go" is echoed often in Scripture as an encouragement to God's servants (cf. Jer. 1:8; Matt. 28:20; Acts 18:10). We should especially note Hebrews 13:5, "For God has said, 'I will never, *never* fail you nor forsake you.'"

Whatever our calling in life, whether teacher, physician, carpenter, secretary, homemaker, God has made provision to strengthen us through the divine resources of his promises and presence. Do you believe this? Then move out by faith into the land God has given you.

Joshua 2:1-24
The Grace of God in an Ancient Hittite City

Key thought: *The trophies of God's grace are where you find them.*

This account is one of the most dramatic and colorful in the book. It is also problematic in the area of ethics on at least two counts: Rahab's occupation and her lying. From his own previous experience as a spy (Num. 13), Joshua wisely dispatched two men to cross the Jordan (evidently by swimming) to investigate Jericho, its fortification, access, and strength. Rahab's house may have been a place of city entertainment and talking, which would provide the spies a likely place to hear any reports about the invading army of Israel as well as a place to escape notice. But they were discovered, and except for the kindness shown by

Rahab in hiding them and lying to the police, they would never have lived to report back to Joshua (v. 12).

This harlot's story is one of redeeming grace. Somehow by the sovereign goodness of God, Rahab the prostitute had been given faith to believe in the God of Israel. She believed his promise to Israel (v. 9); acknowledged his power (v. 10); and in faith confessed his preeminence (v. 11). Her genuine faith is witnessed to by New Testament writers (Heb. 11:31; Jas. 2:25).

Is there not in Rahab an amazing occurrence of divine providence? How else can we explain how two foreigners were guided to a woman in Jericho who trusted in their God and therefore acted kindly to hostile invaders of their land? Was it not also providential for Rahab that of all places in Jericho the men came to her home? His providence is operating just as faithfully today in your life as over 3,000 years ago for Rahab (Rom. 8:28). Are you aware of it?

Some believe that a lie is always a sin and should never be adopted as a course of Christian action. What about Rahab's lie? Did God in his mercy forgive Rahab because of her faith? Or was she justified in lying to save the life of these servants of God? Christians disagree over the way to view the decision made when two of God's laws seem to conflict. Let all of us be persuaded in our own hearts in whatever action we take and in the manner we view our final choice before God.

May we remember the mercy of God extended to this ancient Hittite woman and never underestimate the rich forgiveness of God available to us.

Joshua 3:1–17
D-Day for Palestine

Key thought: *Faith untested is only theoretical faith.*

Preparations all completed, Joshua got the word he was waiting for: "Today," the Lord told Joshua, "I will give you great honor, so that all Israel will know that I am with you just as I was with Moses" (v. 7). Times ahead were going to be anything but easy for Israel. It was absolutely essential that they learn to walk by faith if they were to succeed in claiming the promised land. Now the moment of the supreme test of faith had arrived. Once the Jordan River had been crossed there would be no turning back, no retreat, but only continual battling until victory was won. Several unusual circumstances and proceedings attended this miracle, no doubt to impress on Israel's heart that God was indeed with them and would fulfill his Word to them (v. 10).

The Jordan River normally was about 100 feet wide and three to ten feet deep east of Jericho, but it was at flood stage now (v. 14). No one knew at this point how they were going to get across. They moved the camp to the banks of the Jordan solely by faith (v. 1). Notice how the ark of the covenant is made prominent by repeated references (vv. 3, 6, 8, 11, 13, 14, 15, 17). While in the wilderness the cloud was the symbol of God's leadership over them. Now they were to follow the ark as the visible symbol of God's presence and covenant with them. The instructions were designed to test their faith and obedience. As soon as the feet of the priests among the Levites—it was usually only the Kohathites, not the priests, who carried the ark (cf. Num. 4:15)—were immersed in the muddy waters of the Jordan, a striking miracle occurred, allowing the

Day **3**

Israelites to proceed on the dry riverbed. Miracles are warp and woof of the weaving together of God's Word. They provide unmistakable evidence to God's people of the existence and power of a Being who reveals himself and enters into the affairs of men and history.

Two lessons emerge for us from this signal event in Joshua's day. One is the preeminence of the Lordship of Christ in the Christian life. As the ark was second to no one or no thing, so Christ is to receive first place in every thought and venture in our daily lives. To preempt his place from the center is to spell spiritual disaster. The other lesson is hard to learn. If we would see spiritual power in our lives, we must move out in faith on God's promises (Heb. 11). Faith says, "Get going and keep going." Are you moving?

Joshua 4:1–24
Lest We Forget

Key thought: *A faith that goes all the way with God leaves many beautiful memorials in its wake.* J. SIDLOW BAXTER

This account is the conclusion of the previous event. Two sets of memorial stones were to commemorate the mighty act of God in cutting off the waters of Jordan before the ark of the covenant (v. 7). One of the cairns or monumental piles of twelve stones (one for each tribe) was erected in the river itself at the spot where the priests' feet had rested (v. 9), another on the west bank of the river, at Gilgal (v. 3). The first set was a reminder of the place where God's power was manifested in the miracle. The second was to remind them of what the Lord through his faithfulness had done for them. This witness to Israel's faith and God's power was to be a perpetual encouragement—encouragement not only to the people of Israel, "that all of you will worship him forever" (v. 24), but to their children ("In the future when your children ask you"—v. 21), and to the whole world ("that all the nations of the earth will realize that Jehovah is the mighty God"—v. 24).

God's children in ancient days often erected a memorial to commemorate some special act or revelation of God to them; thus Jacob's meeting God at Bethel (Gen. 28:18, 22; 35:14), or Samuel's victory over the Philistines ("Ebenezer"—1 Sam. 7:10–12). In our day this seems to be a lost practice. Instead we memorialize men rather than the mighty works of God.

Two applications stand out from this chapter. One is the holy practice of frequently reviewing the past, not for our achievements or failures, but for evidences of God's power and faithfulness in our lives. We should close each day by a review of God's dealings with us (Psa. 139:17, 18). Then too, let us not neglect the memorial table of the Lord—"For every time you eat . . ."—given to us by our Savior to remind us of the redeeming love and terrible pathos of the Cross. The other is the sobering thought that the lives of individuals leaving "memorials in their wake" are the lives of men and women who stepped out by faith into God's will. "Self" must be set aside on the eastern bank and Christ embraced by faith as Lord of all.

Joshua 5:1–12
Consecration

Key thought: *Consecration must precede conquest.*

When Israel had by faith crossed the Jordan and had shown their willingness once again to embrace the covenants of Abraham (Gen. 12; 15) and of Moses (Ex. 19) by their obedience in circumcision, the Lord declared that "today I have ended your shame of not being circumcised" (v. 9). For forty years the people were living in disobedience to the covenants by not going into the land promptly when they could have (cf. Num. 13:26ff.). During this period they had desired the things of Egypt (Exod. 16:3; Num. 11:5, 18) and become idolatrous (Ex. 32). For this apostasy the Lord had not allowed them to place the seal of the covenants upon their children (vv. 6, 7). But a new day for Israel had dawned. They had just stepped out in an act of faith and crossed over into their land. Their dedication was to be met by several acts of consecration on God's part. He gave them a new position by circumcision (vv. 8, 9); a new beginning in the third observance of the Passover (v. 10); a new food (vv. 11, 12); and a new Captain (vv. 13–15).

Circumcision was perpetually to represent their separation and new position before the Lord in obedience to his covenant. Crossing Jordan was not enough. Our full surrender to God's purpose for our lives (Rom. 12:1) must be followed by continual daily pruning process of the lusts of the flesh (Rom. 8:12, 13). So many Christians, however, either are attempting to carry out what is represented by Gilgal without having been through the Jordan experience, or have never gone on to Gilgal having once wholly yielded their lives to the Lordship of Christ. Jordan must be followed by

Gilgal. It is painful at first to prune off certain habits of the flesh. But the wound is quickly healed in the balm of the thrilling fellowship of an intimate and satisfying walk with Christ (typified by the Passover feast and the rich corn diet of the land). One final lesson lay just ahead for Joshua before the great enterprise of faith could begin.

Joshua 5:13–15
The Commander in Chief

Key thought: *If Christ is not Lord of everything, he is Lord of nothing.*

Joshua must have quivered as he personally reconnoitered the stronghold of Jericho (v. 13). Suddenly he saw a man with outstretched sword who identified himself as general of the Lord's army. "Take off your shoes," he said, "for this is holy ground" (v. 15). Facing the preincarnate Christ, Joshua had to learn the lesson that he was not the one in charge of the operation that lay ahead. This was no vision, but an actual encounter with the Son of God in human appearance in his preincarnate days—a theophany (an appearance of God). This truth will be taken up later in connection with Samson's birth (Judges). "With a drawn sword ..." (v. 13) was probably a sign to Joshua that he was ready to smite the doomed city of Jericho.

But though Joshua did not perceive the significance of his visitor, thinking him simply to be another ally or foe, he was abruptly confronted with the truth that this One was not another helper but the heavenly Commander himself. The campaign ahead was not his battle but the Lord's. Of course he knew this, but he had to be reminded in such a way that the truth was indelibly impressed upon him. In it lay the secret of success in subjecting and possessing the land the Lord had given.

Here is the secret to the fulfillment of God's purposes for our life. Christ is not simply to be a helper, aiding us in pursuing our goals in life, but he is to be the Commander in Chief of the totality of our life. "Give your bodies to God. Let them be a living sacrifice ... don't copy the behavior and customs of this world, but be a new and different person." The same truth sounds in the words of Paul (Rom. 12:1, 2).

Though he had been a Christian for a number of years, a policeman friend of mine recently discovered the revolutionary experience of completely turning his life over to let Christ run it. God became so real to him in everyday experiences that he remarked, "I have found that you don't have to be a 'member of the cloth' to serve Christ." To prove the reality of the Lord's control over our whole life, we need only to begin the day by acknowledging his ownership of us, ask him to use us, and then thank him for hearing.

Joshua 6:1–27
The Walls of Jericho

Key thought: *God's work must be done in God's way by God's people.*

In the following chapters (6–12) we find the military conquest of Canaan by Israel. Three major campaigns result in the subjection of the whole land. Jericho held the key to the central portion of Canaan and controlled three passes from the Jordan to the central plateau.

Joshua didn't need to devise a plan to capture Jericho because the Lord had his plan already in mind: "I have given them [Jericho and its king and all its mighty warriors] to you." A strange strategy began to be unfolded by God which involved the marching of armed men and priests dressed in white tunics and blowing rams' horns, followed by the ark of the covenant and a rear guard. For six days the city was encircled once each day by this strange, silent entourage. On the seventh day the spectacle was repeated seven times, a shout was given, and the wall of the city miraculously crumbled before the men who invaded and destroyed the city. It must have taken two to three hours to encircle the city seven times on that last day, and the walls were just as strong when they marched around the last time as they were the first day.

Now what is the lesson in this? There was first of all a lesson for Joshua as he learned that the Lord himself was indeed the Commander in Chief. The ark, not Joshua, was the center of the operation. God's plan, not Joshua's strategy, overcame the city. What a lesson for him in trust and obedience!

There was a lesson also for the heathen in the longsuffering of God. Day after day they must have

Day **5**

pondered their fate and thought (as Rahab had) of the reports of Israel's God. None of them needed to perish.

Israel herself was also to learn the lesson of faith. By repeating the marching operation so many times, the people were impressed with their need to trust in God's word and to obey his plans. Israel's faith was the key to their victory. Hebrews 11 records this truth: "It was faith that brought the walls of Jericho tumbling down after the people of Israel had walked around them seven days." Faith evidences its reality in undeviating obedience to God's Word.

Joshua 7:1–26
The Defeat at Ai

Key thought: *Sin lurks in the shadow of faith's victory; like leaven, it soon contaminates the whole.* JOHN REA

Chapter 6 was a story of obedience, victory, and gladness. Before us now lies a story of disobedience, defeat, and gloom. We are immediately informed of the trouble (v. 1) so that we will understand the defeat that follows. Achan, a soldier in the Israelite army, had taken several items of booty from the debris of Jericho and hidden them under the floor of his tent. Soon after, the Israelites advanced against the fortified city of Ai about fifteen miles west of Jericho and had to retreat after about thirty-five men were killed. Dismay struck the army (vv. 2–5). Joshua went to the Lord and blamed him for the defeat (vv. 6–9), whereupon the Lord patiently revealed the source of powerlessness (vv. 10–15). Through an indignant accumulation of verbs, God put his finger on the trouble spot: "Israel has sinned ... disobeyed ... taken loot ... lied about it and hidden it among their belongings" (v. 11). Israel could not stand because the Lord was no longer with them (v. 12). The guilty one would be identified in a public fashion to emphasize the enormity of the sin's effect upon the community. Notice Achan's sad words: "I *saw* [the eye] . . . I *wanted* [the heart] . . . and I *took* [the hand]" (v. 21). Achan, his possessions, and his children were all destroyed in the valley of Achor (vv. 25, 26). His wife is not mentioned, either because she was dead or not involved in the plot.

Two messages strike us from this incident. First, we see that to compromise with sin vitiates the power of God in an individual life. Christian vitality depends upon the immediate energizing of the Spirit of God (Eph. 5:18; Gal. 5:16, 25). This is insured to every believer by his faith, providing he does not "cause the Holy Spirit sorrow" (Eph. 4:30) by tolerating sin in his life. When specific wrong is unconfessed and unforsaken in a Christian's life, the Holy Spirit's personal relationship to that man or woman is strained and he withdraws the special benefits of his presence and power. "If you carefully examine yourselves . . . you will not need to be judged and punished . . . by the Lord" (1 Cor. 11:31, 32).

Second, Achan's covetousness was his own sin but it affected the power of God in the whole group of Israel. Consider the parallel incident in the New Testament of Ananias and Sapphira (Acts 5).

Joshua 8:1–35
The Victory at Ai

Key thought: *Faith is rekindled and reempowered after confession and restored communion with God.*

We find in the eventual defeat of Ai a pattern similar to the victory over Jericho and a direct contrast with the preceding chapter. Disobedience leads to defeat and discouragement (ch. 7), but obedience to God brings victory and joy. The same people battling against the same enemy on the first occasion "were soundly defeated" (7:4). On the other hand, "when the army of Israel had finished slaughtering all the men outside the city, they went back and finished off everyone left inside" (8:24). The lesson of obedience to God's Word is clear. Further, we see faith rekindled and reempowered after confession and return to the Lord.

Joshua then proceeded to "build an altar," to "carve upon the stones of the altar each of the Ten Commandments," and to "read to them all of the statements of blessing and curses that Moses had written in the book of God's laws. Every commandment Moses had ever given ..." (vv. 30–35). In the wake of victory, the temptation often arises to neglect being watchful. The price of freedom is eternal vigilance. This is true of human relations and also of our relation to God. We cannot neglect the place of worship or the place of the Word of God. Worship involves our constant adoration, thanksgiving, confession, and supplication before the Lord. Such respect burns brightly only in hearts ablaze with the Word of the Living God. God's Word sought as daily sustenance by the believer provides a constant deterrent to pride of accomplishment and neglect of dependence upon the

Day **6**

Lord. These basic means of grace to the soul are neglected to one's own spiritual peril. Even "the women, and the children, and the foreigners who lived among the Israelis" (v. 35) were commanded to listen to the Word of God. Put the altar and the Bible first in your life today and God will fill your life with his presence and fullness (read Eph. 3:16–19). Faith, then, burns brightest when it has been kindled afresh each day by holy worship and meaningful consideration of the Word of God.

How do you read Scripture? Do you read only for encouragement and blessing? If you overlook the fact that the Bible contains both "blessing and *curses* (v. 34), you may fail to be adequately warned of your faults and thus unable to grow. A burning lamp must not only have the oil of God's blessing but the trimmed wick of self-judgment. Let your Bible meditation encourage you but let it also daily judge you.

Joshua 8:32–35
The Integrity of the Scriptures

Key thought: *Forever, O Lord, your Word stands firm in heaven.* PSA. 119:89

During the nineteenth century a system of theology developed that attempted to harmonize Christian theology with the diverse elements of the so-called new learning. This system is identified under several names, but is probably best known as liberalism or modernism. We pause to discuss this movement here because of Joshua's references to the "law of Moses" in the verses before us. Since informed Christians are forewarned and forearmed Christians, such a discussion seems appropriate to our study.

In the enthusiasm of the civilized world over the discoveries of Copernicus (d. 1543), Galileo (d. 1642), and Newton (d. 1727), which led to the rise of modern science, there also developed simultaneously, but not always in association, a naturalistic philosophy of life. This claimed that nature was all there was and excluded anything supernatural from the universe. The scientific method, it was said, yielded the only valid way of obtaining knowledge. Since miracles are not scientifically verifiable (because not repeatable), liberalism much later sought to reinterpret the miraculous prophecy; it had to postulate dates and authors for books that were considerably later than Scripture claims, thereby making the prophecies simply "apparent" prophecies. In this view, prophecies were written by people who lived *after* the events had taken place. This approach was coupled with a second, equally devastating and equally erroneous hypothesis about the evolution of religion. The earliest form of religion was assumed to be animism (worship of elemental spirits), which developed into polytheism (many gods), and finally into monotheism (one god). Therefore, any sections of the Pentateuch or Joshua, etc., that contain references to monotheistic worship must have been added by later writers after religion had evolved into this form. Both of these hypotheses are without evidence to support them, and they undermine the plain statements and claims of eyewitnesses who wrote the biblical records. The reader is referred to a splendid recent work by a competent evangelical scholar who has unquestionably refuted these erroneous allegations (*A Survey of Old Testament Introduction* by Gleason Archer).

If Joshua "read to them all of the statements of blessing and curses that Moses had written in the book of God's laws" (v. 34), we can rest assured that a written law of Moses was in existence by Joshua's time. There is no reason to question the authority of the record.

Joshua 9:1–27
Compromise with Gibeon

Key thought: *We need not only the power of the Spirit against giants, but the wisdom of the Spirit against serpents.* J. SIDLOW BAXTER

Situated about six and one-half miles southwest of Ai, Gibeon was the capital of an independent republic ruled by elders rather than a king (v. 11). Gibeonites may well have been the ancient Hurrians, a dominant ethnic group in Palestine especially in the sixteenth and fifteenth centuries B.C.

Since the Gibeonites had heard of the divine commission given to Israel to destroy all the inhabitants of Palestine, they devised a clever plan to secure a pact of protection from the invading nation. Dressed in old clothes, and carrying mended wineskins and moldy bread, they made out as if they had traveled a great distance from a far country. Since Israel's orders were to destroy only the Canaanites and not distant lands (Deut. 20:10–18), they were beguiled by Gibeon to covenant not to kill them. Within a short time the deception was uncovered, but not soon enough to avert a hasty and binding oath made by Israel with the Gibeonites. Joshua had fallen prey to the sin of excessive credulity and rashness. Striking this time not through head-long armed resistance but through the subtlety of a pity-evoking beggar's attire, Satan caused Israel's faith to be endangered through compromise.

The key to the lesson seems to be in the short but stinging rebuke, "They did not bother to ask the Lord, but went ahead and signed a peace treaty" (v. 14). Satan came in his crafty strategems (Eph. 6:11), as an angel of light (2 Cor. 11:14, 15). Faith was thrown off guard because it was ignorant of his methods

(2 Cor. 2:11). Our chief defense against the devil's craft is the resource of prayer and trust in God. Our heavenly Father alone knows the many subtleties of the archenemy of our faith and we must learn to seek his leading at every juncture of our life. God has unconditionally promised to supply wisdom in temptations to those who ask in simple, unhesitating faith (Jas. 1:5, 6).

Satan may this day come to you in subtlety as an angel of light. Because you have this word from God out of Joshua's experience, you need not be excessively credulous or rash in your decision. Seek the Lord's advice and have some sure word from him.

Joshua 10:1–14
The Day the Sun Stood Still

Key thought: *More things are wrought by prayer than this world dreams of.* ALFRED TENNYSON IN IDYLLS OF THE KING

With word spreading of Israel's victories, it was inevitable that the surrounding nations in Canaan would call a parlay and ally together against the invading army. Gibeon, endangered because of her treaty with Israel, appealed to Joshua for help. The resultant battle is one of the most significant in history. In the words of the record, "There had never been such a day before, and there has never been another since. . . . But the Lord was fighting for Israel" (v. 14). Two miracles are recorded in connection with the defeat of the Amorites. A great hailstorm occurred as the enemy was retreating and killed a large number of the troops (v. 11). Then, in response to Joshua's prayer, the Lord performed one of the most amazing miracles recorded in history (vv. 12–14). This miracle of the sun standing still has been called by some "the most striking incidence of science and Scripture being at variance." However, none but extreme rationalists would deny that a notable miracle occurred. Just how we are to understand what actually happened remains more of a problem.

In the first place the Bible affirms that "the sun and the moon didn't move until the Israeli army had finished the destruction of its enemies" (v. 13). Now, since the time of Copernicus it has been known that the earth revolves around the sun and not vice versa. Whatever happened in the miracle, the sun did not stop because it doesn't revolve around the earth. It is foolish, however, on this basis to impugn the Bible for inaccuracy. The Bible is written in phenomenal language or the universal language of appearance. Hence, "the sun rises" or "the sun sets" is perfectly accurate language (as in the *Naval Almanac*) from the standpoint of appearance. It appeared to those in Gibeon that the sun stood still on that day. Whether God caused the earth to stop rotating (or slow down), or produced a miracle of light refraction similar to the northern lights, or caused the sun to cease to give off its heat on Gibeon as some have thought, remains incidental to the fact that God supernaturally intervened in behalf of his people in answer to prayer. Let us never limit God by our lack of faith in prayer.

Joshua 11:1–23
The Northern Campaign

Key thought: *If God is on our side, who can ever be against us? . . . He used God's mighty weapons, not those made by man, to knock down the devil's strongholds.* PAUL THE APOSTLE

Joshua's plan was now clear. He had driven a wedge into the center of the country by striking Jericho (chap. 6) and Ai (chap. 8), then marched southward to Makkedah, Libnah, Lachish, Eglon, Hebron, and Debir (10:28–39). Now he would turn northward to the powerful confederacy summoned by Jabin, king of Hazor, at Merom (11:1ff.). Joshua moved so swiftly and struck so unexpectedly that the kings were caught off guard and were defeated.

According to first-century Jewish historian Josephus, there were 300,000 infantrymen, 10,000 cavalry troops, and 20,000 chariots (used in battles in the lowlands) in this massing of enemy forces. Joshua "attacked" them, "chased" them, "hamstrung" the horses, and "burned" their chariots with fire (vv. 7–9). "Hamstringing" was an ancient tactic of cutting the back leg tendons of the horses, thus disabling them for warfare but allowing them to be serviceable for agricultural purposes. Chapter 12 then records the military log of the thirty-one kings and lands that fell before Joshua and Israel. Every united effort against Israel proved to no avail because God was in the battle for his people. It was not, however, an easy battle nor a short one. "It took seven years of war to accomplish all of this" (v. 18).

In such a context we can see that the Christian warfare (Eph. 6:12, 13) likewise requires an active, persistent application of our physical, mental,

Day 8

emotional, and spiritual reserves to the day-by-day battle. Paul describes a twofold working as he admonishes the Philippians to "do the good things that result from being saved, obeying God with deep reverence, shrinking back from all that might displease him" (not work *for* but work *out* in its implications), for "God is at work within you, helping you want to obey him, and then helping you do what he wants" (Phil. 2:12, 13). Let us not confuse the diligent application of all our faculties to Christian living with laboring in the flesh. To labor in the flesh involves an attitude of self-centeredness. To labor in the Spirit involves the same effort and work but with an attitude of Christ-centeredness and reliance upon the power of God (1 Cor. 10:31). With such an attitude all that you undertake today can be brought under his dominion.

Joshua 6:21; 8:26; 11:11
Extermination of the Canaanites

Key thought: *See how God is both so kind and so severe. He is very hard on those who disobey, but very good to you.* PAUL THE APOSTLE

The question of the command to exterminate the Canaanites is often raised by thoughtful non-Christians and Christians alike. We have noticed earlier in the book of Joshua such statements as "They destroyed everything in it—men, and women, young and old ... everything" (6:21); and "Joshua kept his spear pointed toward Ai until the last person was dead" (8:26; 11:11). How do you justify Israel's extermination of every inhabitant of these cities? Where is their mercy? In some quarters this act is explained as an atrocity performed by "primitive-minded, half-savage" Israelites in their backward state of religious development. But such an answer does not satisfy those who rightly hold to the integrity of the biblical documents. In a brief sketch we may outline a more satisfactory answer.

1. It must be emphasized that God commanded such a procedure and the responsibility is with him and not the Israelites (cf. Deut. 20:16, 17).

2. Repeatedly in the Bible God is revealed as One who visits judgment upon the sin of individuals and nations including his people Israel (cf. Amos 1, 2). If God can destroy his own people because of their sin and unbelief (cf. Isa. 10:5ff.; Hab. 1:6ff.) by using a more wicked people as an instrument, can he not also destroy a corrupt and rebellious people by using Israel? The question, then, is not how could a God of love do it, but how could a God of justice delay?

3. Archaeology has revealed that Canaan's religion was crass and brutal. Ras Shamra literature reveals at least seventy gods in Canaan. The people were eager to incorporate every new god into their religion, which would make the monotheism of the Israelites practically impossible under such circumstances. The crudest form of sexual perversion and temple prostitution apparently accompanied the religious rites. Infant sacrifice was practiced.

Thus the command of God to exterminate the Canaanites may be partially understood as an act of judgment upon spiritual apostasy.

Joshua 13–24
Distribution of the Land

Key thought: *God's promises are the title deed to all of his inheritance.*

The great enterprise undertaken by Joshua is summarized in chapter 11, verse 23. "So Joshua took the entire land ... and he gave it to the people of Israel as their inheritance." This verse provides a literary pivot or hinge for the book. Joshua "took" the land (chs. 1–12), and Joshua "gave" or divided the land for Israel (chs. 13–24). The remainder of the book, then, deals primarily with the distribution of the land among the twelve tribes. These chapters are filled with names, places, and boundary lines and yield little spiritual profit to the casual reader. Tucked in and almost hidden, however, lie a number of special lessons for us. Some of these will be noted in the following studies. We can, though, make some general observations here.

1. Chapters 13 through 17 are occupied with the land distribution to the tribes of Reuben, Gad, Manasseh and Judah, while chapters 18 and 19 relate the establishment of the tabernacle in Shiloh and the settlement of the remaining seven tribes.

2. The tribe of Levi received no land allotment, because they were the priestly tribe and their inheritance was to be the offerings brought to the Lord by the Israelites (13:14; 18:7; 21:1f.).

3. Though distribution was settled by the "throwing of dice" (18:6), it was not caprice. Principles were also employed, such as the capacity of the tribe (17:16); the priority of conquest (17:14, 17); God's providence (13:6); request (Num. 32:1–5); privilege (21:3); claim (15:9); and faithfulness (14:13, 14).

Day 9

4. The occupation of the land was not immediate nor complete even though the division was made by Joshua.

5. In addition to the tribal allotments, cities of refuge for the manslayer were assigned (20:1f.).

6. The entire process was complex and required much time and consideration.

Above all these considerations was the reward of faith. God promised Israel the land (1:2–6), and they received the land because they believed God. We must now consider the principle of faith-possession more in detail.

Joshua 13:1; 18:1–6; 21:43–45
Possessing Our Possessions

Key thought: *Faith translates inheritance into possessions.*

We cannot leave the matter of Israel's receiving the land without considering the principle on which she was able to do it. This principle can be seen by comparing two apparently contradictory statements in 11:23 and 13:1. The former states that Israel "took the entire land," while the latter reminds Joshua in his advanced age that "there are still many nations to be conquered." These statements are not really contradictory but complementary. They reveal two important aspects of the same truth. On the one hand, decisive and major victories had been won that insured ultimate victory; on the other hand, the details and mopping-up operations had to be pressed to provide a permanent inheritance.

Here is a vital lesson for the Christian life of faith. Perhaps you have experienced by faith the redeeming love of Christ in the forgiveness of your sin, a newfound joy and peace and guidance for your life, yet you have not moved out by faith to see all of the land of God's provision "occupied" in your experience. You know nothing of victory over enslaving habits of indolence, triviality, gossip, jealousy, anger, pride. Or perhaps if you have known victory you have soon capitulated and given up the land once occupied by faith. In his book *Spiritual Depression, Its Causes and Cure,* D. Martyn Lloyd-Jones makes the observation that holiness is not something received in a meeting. Rather it is a life to be lived and to be lived in detail. Have we forgotten the details of this life? Has indifference been our chief enemy in possessing all the "blessings in the heavenlies" that Christ has victoriously won for us in his death?

Faith is related closely to an act of the will. We determine before God to apply his provisions of grace to every detail of our thought and life (18:1–6). Jesus Christ wants our will—totally, unreservedly yielded to him. Today you may possess more of your inheritance by claiming it by faith (read 21:43–45).

Joshua 14:6–14
Caleb's Testimony

Key thought: *They that wait upon the Lord shall renew their strength . . . they shall run, and not be weary.* THE PROPHET ISAIAH

In connection with the rather mundane notices of the property divisions to the tribe of Judah, a brief but thrilling biographical sketch of Caleb is included. He was now eighty-five years old and it had been forty-five years since he courageously spied out the land of Canaan and brought back a report of faith along with Joshua (Num. 13). Even in old age his zeal and courage and strength had not waned. He requested permission to take the stronghold of Hebron from the Anakim (v. 12) and proceeded to do what he had claimed he could (15:14).

Caleb is an example of a life under the control of the Lord. This passage attributes his success in life to the fact that he "followed the Lord, his God" (vv. 8, 14). What does such an expression mean? Literally Caleb said, "I have filled up after the Lord." The figure of speech is taken from the activity of hunting wild animals. As the hunter tracks his prey, he gradually closes up the distance between himself and the animal until he overtakes and seizes the catch. Caleb says that he has filled up the gap between the footprints of the Lord and his own. He has pursued closely the tracks of his God through his life. Peter paints a similar picture of our relationship to Christ Jesus. "This suffering is all part of the work God has given you. Christ, who suffered for you, is your example. Follow in his steps" (1 Pet. 2:21). Through his Word and prayer we can know where his path winds through life. As we obey

Day 10

we will find the gap between him and us gradually filling in. Here we see the devotion of faith.

How refreshing to find an old man like Caleb who is alive to God and still winning battles for his Savior. Time is no enemy to the certain fulfillment of God's promises (cf. 2 Pet. 3:8, 9). Happy are all those who "renew their strength" day after day, year after year by "looking expectantly" to a God who never fails to keep his promises, whose faithfulness is as high as the heavens are above the earth.

Joshua 20:1–9
The Cities of Refuge

Key thought: *Mistakes are not sins.*

Now when they had "supervised the sacred lottery to divide the land among the tribes" (19:51), Joshua received commandment to appoint six cities of refuge for the offense of manslaying. If a person had inadvertently killed someone, without premeditation, he could flee for asylum to one of the appointed cities. After his case was approved, he was granted protection from anyone seeking his life. Then a trial was held near the scene of the crime. If he was innocent, he could return to the city of refuge. After the death of the high priest in office, he was permitted to return to his home. Such was the gracious provision of the Lord for an unintentional wrong (cf. Exod. 21:12–14; Num. 35:1–34). Two lessons for us can be seen in this appointment of God in ancient Israel.

We see first of all that God recognizes a difference between *sins* and *mistakes*. The most godly and upright among us are fallible and frequently make mistakes; but mistakes are not sins and therefore they don't cut us off from the divine fellowship nor grieve the Holy Spirit within us. The difference is in "knowing what is right to do and then not doing it" (Jas. 4:17). My two-year-old daughter who threw her new shoes into a bathtub full of water one day had made a mistake, but had not committed a sin. "A man may have a perfect heart without having a perfect head. Sanctification can dwell with a defective memory. Let us be quick to perceive such distinctions and compatibilities" (J. Sidlow Baxter).

Some, also, see a type of Christ in these cities. Such a passage as "All those who flee to him to save them can take new courage when they hear such assurances from God" (Heb. 6:18) seems to echo this truth (cf. Psa. 46:1; Rom. 8:1). There is provision for our mistakes as well as our sins in the refuge of Christ's blood (1 John 1:9).

"Hidden in the hollow of his blessed hand/ Never foe can follow, never traitor stand/ Not a surge of worry, not a shade of care/ Not a blast of hurry touch the spirit there./ Stayed upon Jehovah, hearts are fully blest/ Finding as he promised, perfect peace and rest."

Joshua 22:10–34
The Altar "Ed"

Key thought: *The acid test of grace lies not in whether our enemies are all subdued but in whether we can get along with our friends.*

When the two and a half tribes returned from Shiloh and from helping their brother tribes capture their lands, they decided to set up an attractive altar on the western side of the Jordan River to remind their children and the children of the rest of the nation westward that they also were part of the Lord's inheritance. As soon as news reached the rest of the congregation of Israel in Canaan, they were infuriated at what the two and a half tribes had done. Thinking they had apostasized from the Lord in building another altar, which was forbidden by Moses, the rest of Israel was ready to go to war and destroy them all (v. 12).

How pathetic, but how typical! Having enjoyed the great victory of the Lord's working for them in subduing Canaan, they now turned to destroy one another. The near disaster could have been avoided. The altar was unnecessary, since they were to appear anyway three times a year at Shiloh to sacrifice and worship (Exod. 23:14). Perhaps it was even presumptuous because the Lord had not directed such a venture. There are at least two lessons for us in this schismatic altar "Ed" ("witness"—v. 34).

In the first place, the incident illustrates the folly of judging another's motives on the basis of his outward actions. An action often is capable of a dozen different explanations. We tend to jump too quickly to the conclusion that a fellow Christian has erred or departed from loyalty to Christ when we hear of something he has done. In this incident the motives,

Day 11

though misleading, were apparently pure. Only the Lord himself can judge another's actions because he knows all the circumstances and motives (1 Cor. 4:5).

Second, this incident illustrates the folly of trying to establish unity by some outward maneuver. Unity rests upon discovery of oneness of life and spiritual experience in Christ which has already been established for us by the powerful agency of the Holy Spirit (Eph. 4:3–5). We cannot make unity, but we can "keep" (observe) the unity already made.

Joshua 23:1–16
Joshua's First Farewell Address

Key thought: *Just as definite laws insure the continuous operation of the physical universe, so inviolable principles govern our continuing spiritual life.*

We come now to the parting words of the aged Joshua who must have been over one hundred years old at this time. The faithful leader bared his burdened heart concerning the future of the nation. Everything depended upon whether Israel would keep God's covenant. Seven times their leader referred to the danger from the heathen nations left in the land, whose gods would ensnare Israel and bring down upon them the wrath of God unless they were vigilant in spiritual matters (vv. 7, 12, 13, 16). Joshua's instruction to save them from apostasy involved three specific activities. First, and most important, they were to be diligently concerned with keeping the Word of God without any compromise in their obedience (v. 6). Then, they must keep themselves separate from evil by total isolation from these remaining nations (v. 7). Finally, they must be devoted to the Lord their God in a genuine and fervent love (vv. 8, 11).

These three basic conditions for God's continuing blessing upon his people are as important today as for Joshua's day. In the life that knows the ever-increasing blessing of God's presence and provision, there is (1) hunger for and attention to the Word of God, the Bible; (2) separation from all known evil in the life; and (3) commitment to Jesus Christ that is in essence a passionate love for him. One cannot help thinking of Jude's exhortation with practically the same emphasis. "But you, dear friends, must build up your lives ever more strongly upon the foundation of our holy faith, learning to pray in the power and strength of the Holy Spirit. Stay always within the boundaries where God's love can reach and bless you. Wait patiently for the eternal life that our Lord Jesus Christ in his mercy is going to give you" (Jude 20, 21) In a day of many unbalanced approaches to Christian separation, one needs constantly the orientation to the pure scriptural emphasis.

The Word of God admonishes us to separate ourselves not from the world of men, but from the evil of the world. We must assiduously cultivate a vital and positive personal relationship with the Lord Jesus, immersing ourselves in his love and fortifying our being with his life and grace. Living close to the Word, consistent separation from any sin, and daily cultivating a personal love relationship with Jesus Christ are God's laws to sustain our spiritual well-being.

Joshua 24:1–33
Joshua's Final Farewell

Key thought: *God is still waiting to see deeper commitment among his people than can be found today.*

The final chapter is composed of three movements. In the first, Joshua reviewed the blessings of the nation —beginning with the call of Abraham and the birth of the patriarchs and extending to the deliverance out of Egyptian bondage under Moses, God's faithfulness in the wilderness, the events related to the entrance into Canaan, and the consequent victory under Joshua. Thus, Israel was reminded of the Lord's goodness and blessing in days gone past (vv. 1–13).

The burden on Joshua's heart is revealed in the stirring dialogue of the second movement (vv. 14–28). Five times Joshua exhorted the people to serve the Lord and depart from the entrapment of foreign gods, and four times the people affirmed, "We will serve the Lord." The tone of Joshua's words leads us to suspect that he detected a glibness in the people's affirmations of service. Notice how he said, "Serve him in sincerity and truth" (v. 14), "Decide today whom you will obey" (v. 15), and "You can't worship the Lord God . . . he will not forgive your rebellion and sins" (v. 19).

In our day also many believers have made a semblance of dedication, but lack deep devotion to our Lord Jesus Christ. It is one of the church's main problems. What do we know of such devotion as "Let goods and kindred go, this mortal life also" or "I have worked harder, been put in jail oftener, been whipped times without number, and faced death again and again and again" (2 Cor. 11:23ff.)? Ours is an age of spiritual declension. The Word of God calls us to look at our commitment to the Lord by the scriptural

Day **12**

standard of Christ and the apostles. We are to forsake all evil and sin and cultivate a fervent love for him (23:23).

The third movement (vv. 29–33) tells of Joshua's death and Israel's obedience. Joshua's godly influence extended throughout his time until his death and as long as the leaders who knew him lived (v. 31). Thus another segment of God's unfolding plan of redemption draws to a close. "Great is thy faithfulness."

PART TWO

JUDGES: FAITH'S TRIUMPH IN TIME OF DECLENSION

INTRODUCTION TO JUDGES

Joshua is dead. The land is occupied. The challenge is over and the people turn to folly.

It is one thing to live for God when there is a blazing frontier at each new daybreak. It is quite another to follow him when the days are routine and the land is settled.

Compared with the "pioneer" spirit in Joshua, Judges is a book of the "settlers." Both times are to be confronted with faith. In one sense it is more difficult to live victoriously in routine than in eventful days. We can learn from the episodes in this unusual Old Testament book.

Joshua was a book focusing on one man. It pictured a united people, and contained only ripples of failure. Judges unfolds as a record of many men, a divided people, and wave after wave of failure. Why would God give us such a book? Certainly it was written to instruct us in the ancient pitfalls of mankind and to challenge us by the lives of men and women who moved against the tide of corruption around them. Have you met and lived with the heroes Othniel and Ehud, Deborah and Barak, Gideon and Samson? Have you been introduced to the rascal Abimelech or seen the folly of Micah and the Danites? Did you know that things were so bad in this period that a young girl was raped until she was dead and her dismembered body sent throughout Israel?

The words of Robert Robinson's song, "Come, Thou Fount" seem to capture the tone of the book of Judges: "Prone to wander, Lord, I feel it/Prone to leave the God I love." Here is a record of the perpetual propensity of the human heart to leave the God of redeeming love. "The people of Israel again sinned against the Lord" is repeated over and over in this book. The judges were political and spiritual leaders over a period of some 400 years. Through their faith they led the people of Israel during oppression by the surrounding nations from the time of Joshua's death until the birth of the prophet Samuel.

This book traces a dark period of national declension for Israel. We see the reality and causes of failure in lives in covenant relation to the living God.

An outline and occasional reminder of where we are in the book should prove helpful as we look at the scenes in this drama of "faith's triumph in times of declension."

OUTLINE OF JUDGES

I. Causes of the Period (1–3)
   A. Failure to drive out the heathen (1)
   B. Failure to worship Jehovah alone (2)
   C. Failure to marry only believers (3)

II. Conditions of the Period (3–16)
   A. Under Deborah and Barak (3–5)
   B. Under Gideon (6–8)
   C. Abimelech, the "Bramble King" (9, 10)
   D. Under Jephthah (11, 12)
   E. Under Samson (13–16)

III. Consequences of the Period (17–21)
   A. Idolatry of Micah and Danites (17, 18)
   B. Immorality and outrage at Gibeah (19)
   C. Anarchy in Benjamin (20–21)

Take your *Living Bible* and read first each section of Judges before you consult these comments. Remember that this book is only a pointer to the truths of the book of Judges itself.

Judges 21:25
A Period of Declension

Key thought: *The incurable wickedness of the human heart is revealed no more clearly than in its proneness to leave the God it loves.*

We begin in the book of Judges at the back door where the key seems to have been left. From 21:25 the general tone and development of the book can be detected: "There was no king in Israel in those days, and every man did whatever he thought was right." After the death of Joshua's elders, spiritual declension and apostasy soon swept into the nation. Everyone doing as he pleases denotes a lack of authority. It probably involved (as the book shows) political, social, and spiritual rebellion. Hence apostasy is the theme of Judges, and in its chapters we will find illustrated the truth that the human heart is perpetually prone to apostasy. Let us again recall the words of "Come, Thou Fount of Every Blessing": "Let Thy goodness, like a fetter/Bind my wandering heart to Thee/Prone to wander, Lord, I feel it/Prone to leave the God I love." "They did that which was evil in the sight of the Lord" is a phrase occurring seven times in the book.

The book may be viewed from several angles. In the first few chapters we see the *causes* for the period of declension (chs. 1–3), but the majority of the book describes actual *conditions* in the period (chs. 4–16). Finally, in the last five chapters (17–21), we find the *consequences* that this period produced in people's lives. A clinical view would see first the *etiology* of Israel's sickness (1–3), then the *diagnosis* (4–16), and finally the *prognosis* (17–21). These sections, viewed legally, could be called the *charge,* the *case,* and the *evidence.*

Day **13**

Although darkness prevails in this period, brilliant flashes of light also appear in the outstanding examples of faith found in the "judges" or saviors whom God raised up to deliver the people from oppression. Many of the heroes of faith recorded in Hebrews 11 in the New Testament are taken from the pages of the book of Judges. They are lilies in a stagnant pool.

Careful study of this book will say much to us about our own relationship to the Lord. We will come away with joy and profit.

Judges 1:1–36
The Judgment of God

Key thought: *Wholeheartedness is rewarded by the Lord but indecision brings his judgment.*

A glance at this first chapter of Judges reveals that to begin with it contains a catalog of the military conquests of the tribe of Judah in the years after the death of Joshua (vv. 1–21). Following is a summary of the exploits of seven other Israelite tribes as they attempted to subject the land to their rule (vv. 22–36). A cursory reading of the chapter yields little of spiritual interest; it seems rather dull and irrelevant. But a closer look reveals a definite pattern and an obvious division in the material that boldly yields a lesson designedly relevant to our lives. Notice, first, this pattern. In verses 4, 8, 10, 17, and 19 we find references to Judah's going against various Canaanite strongholds and completely conquering the enemy. The Lord delivered the Canaanites and Perizzites into their hand (v. 4, etc.). However, beginning with the tribe of

Benjamin (v. 21) and continuing on through the listings of the other eight tribes mentioned (except Joseph) there is a degeneracy in their success in driving out the heathen nations (cf. "drove not out" in vv. 21, 27, 29, 30, 31, 33, 34). Here the Spirit of God has a message for us. "In later years when the Israelis were stronger they put the Canaanites to work as slaves, but never did force them to leave the country" (v. 28). Failure to decide to obey God at all costs not only left Israel without his help, but needlessly brought his judgment upon them (2:3).

The Lord has established a principle in his dealing with us: if we would enjoy his full provisions, our whole heart must be his. Because of this fact, some Christians sputter through life like a wet match without ever igniting into flame for God. If we would know the thrilling experience of day-by-day victory over the enemies of indifference, dishonesty, discouragement, fear, and pride, let us give as much of ourselves as we can to as much of Christ as we know.

"Only one heart's devotion / Savior, oh, may it be / Consecrated alone to Thy matchless glory/ Yielded fully to Thee."

Judges 2:1–23
The Causes of Failure

Key thought: *A chief source of failure in life is our tolerance of incomplete obedience to God's whole counsel.*

This chapter opens with the touching and instructive incident of the angel of the Lord visiting Israel with reprimanding words (vv. 1–5); it should be regarded as part of chapter one. Probably we are to understand the "angel of the Lord" as the preincarnate Christ appearing in angelic form (see comments on ch. 13). "At Bochim, coming from Gilgal" is not so much a geographical reference as it is spiritual. It was at Gilgal that the Commander-in-Chief of the Lord's army appeared to Joshua as the One who was to be obeyed if they were to have victory at Jericho (Josh. 5:10, 13–15). He had now come from the place of Israel's obedience to the place of their present disobedience, called Bochim or "the place where people wept" (v. 5). They had failed to obey him totally by not driving out the heathen nations and breaking down their altars (v. 2). When their love for him cooled, and they evaded their responsibility, the Lord in judgment would not drive out the idolatrous inhabitants of the land (ch. 1), but left them to stultify Israel's progress and be to them a continual temptation (v. 3). Through this temptation, they sank still lower and served the pagan gods of Canaan. The Lord then allowed them to be taken captive and enslaved by the surrounding nations (vv. 11–15) until in his mercy he raised up a deliverer. Still, "The people turned from doing right. . . . they stubbornly returned to the evil customs of the nations around them" (vv. 16–23). Thus we have the preview of the sad story that the record of Judges will tell.

Day 14

Let us constantly be on our guard against anything, however small, that may take our love away from Jesus Christ. It may be the way we use our leisure time or our reading habits or a favorite chair that we would rather relax in than assemble with our brothers and sisters for worship. When our love cools, we evade our total responsibility to Christ. And God often uses that very thing that took us away from him to afflict us. God doth "of our pleasant vices make instruments to scourge us" (Shakespeare, *King Lear*).

We should be warned by this lesson that God's threats upon backsliders are not empty words. Israel failed because they compromised. Their tolerance of incomplete obedience brought God's hand against them.

Judges 3:7–11
The Sin Cycle and First Judge

Key thought: *While God's love seeks to bless us always, his righteousness binds him to chastise us for our sin.*

After the death of Joshua and his elders, their godly stabilizing influence upon the nation was soon forgotten and "the next generation did not worship Jehovah as their God" (2:10). A pattern begins in chapter 3 that will be repeated seven times during the dismal period of the judges. The pattern is so clear and instructive to our own lives that we must point it out in detail as we consider the first judge, Othniel.

The problem began each time with (1) Israel's *sin*: "So the people of Israel were very evil in God's sight" (v. 7). Then came God's judgment upon them in the form of (2) *servitude* to a heathen people: "And he let King Cushanrishathaim of eastern Syria conquer them" (v. 8). Next Israel in distress eventually turned back to the Lord and pled his grace in (3) *supplication*: "When Israel cried out to the Lord, he gave them Caleb's nephew, Othniel, to save them" (v. 9), and Othniel brought (4) *salvation* from their oppressors (v. 9). Finally there was (5) *silence* in the land from war for a period of time. "For forty years under Othniel, there was peace in the land" (v. 11). So we have sin, servitude, supplication, salvation, and silence. In the sevenfold repetition of this pattern lies the tragedy of the people and the period. Each cycle brought the nation more deeply into sin and internal corruption. Each displayed a combination of God's retribution on their sin, his untiring grace and mercy in repeatedly raising up a deliverer (judge) in response to their cries, and his restoring them to their freedom.

SIN CYCLE

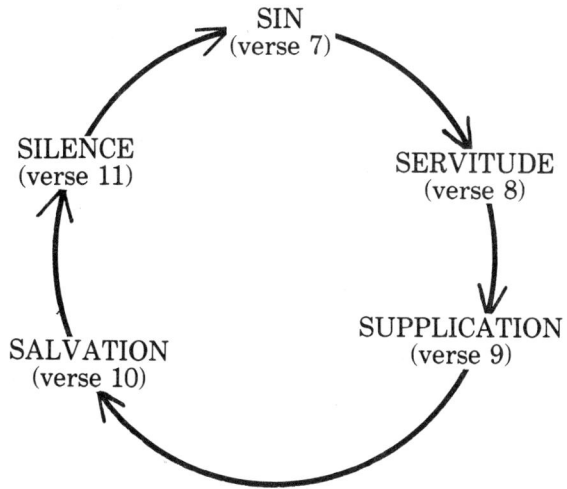

Othniel, Caleb's nephew, was the first such savior or judge (v. 9). These individuals were probably local military leaders, without any line of succession, who were viewed as champions of the people's political and judicial life. Othniel's success was plainly not due to human genius but came because "the Spirit of the Lord took control of him" (v. 10). Around these apostasies and saviors the Holy Spirit weaves a message to our hearts.

Think about this pattern: (1) Sin always brings suffering; (2) privileges from God to us are not privileges to sin; (3) distress and trouble drive us to prayer; (4) hypocrisy means high calling and low living; and (5) compromise brings defeat, but faith gives continual rest.

Judges 3:12–30
How Well Do You Remember?

Key thought: *Lessons learned in adversity should not be forgotten in prosperity.*

Again Israel relapsed into sin and brought the judgment of the Lord upon them (servitude): "For the next eighteen years the people of Israel were required to pay crushing taxes to King Eglon" (v. 14). There is a tragic note in the word *again*. After all they had suffered because of sin, and so soon after their Lord's gracious deliverance under Othniel, they again fell into apostasy. Someone has remarked that "neither ministry nor miracle, nor misery nor mercy, could mollify their hard hearts." We are prone to forget so quickly not only the goodness of the Lord to us, but also the lessons that his chastisement are designed to teach us (2 Pet. 1:9). Then, too, each relapse brings further insensitivity to God's faithful stinging of our conscience because of the sin. An insensitive heart goes deeper into sin before it will repent. We must not refuse the Lord's gentle nudges prompting us to repentance and confession in the early stages of any such forsaking of him; otherwise we are in danger of bringing upon ourselves a spiritual hardening of the heart (Heb. 3:12, 13). Be quick to judge sin in your experience. Make it a daily practice to expose yourself thoroughly before the Lord at the day's end as David did: "Search me, O God, and know my heart; test my thoughts" (Psa. 139:23).

A doctor friend of mine told me recently that the nerves of the body lie very close to the surface of our skin and are therefore highly sensitive to irritation. But this position also makes them vulnerable to

Day **15**

damage, especially from burns which render the nerves completely and permanently insensitive to further stimulation. Isn't our heart like that before the Lord? "Keep thy heart with all diligence, for out of it are the issues of life" (Proverbs).

The memory is a wonderful gift from God, indispensable for a continuing healthy relationship with the Lord. "Think about those times of your first love (how different now!) and turn back to me again" is the admonition of our Lord (Rev. 2:5). We must daily apply it if we would grow in grace and holiness before him.

Judges 4:1–7
Women in God's Service

Key thought: *The world knows no greater force for good than a woman of faith faithful to her calling.*

Israel's next apostasy occurred following Ehud's death. The Lord punished them by bringing them under the servitude of Jabin, king of Canaan, for twenty years until they turned to God. Then he raised up Deborah and Barak to deliver them. Perhaps we should look primarily at the people in this episode and learn something about how human character responds to God's claims.

Deborah was one of a few women in biblical history whom the Lord chose to elevate to a place of special spiritual leadership among his people. She, like Miriam (Exod. 15:20) and Huldah (2 Kgs. 22:14), was a prophetess in the nation, which involved in this case the responsibility of judging civil law cases (v. 5). Deborah seems to be a foreshadowing of the new times to come under Christ. Jesus' attitude toward the importance of women is nothing less than revolutionary for his times. He permitted them to accompany him in his ministry and even to support him financially. Women were the first to see the risen Christ and to report the news of his resurrection to others. They appear as prominent figures in his parables. Some of his most significant teaching was occasioned by conversations with certain women.

Among the first Christian disciples baptized with the Holy Spirit on the day of Pentecost were women. They held the prestigious position in the early church as prophets, like Philip's four daughters, or as deacons, such as Phoebe. Paul at the close of his Roman letter commended a number of women as notable servants of God in the gospel ministry. In keeping with Jesus' attitude the apostles address women in their letters as fully responsible persons.

Women have always held a vital place in God's overall work. Consider also Sarah (Gen. 21), Rebekah (Gen. 24), Lydia (Acts 16), Priscilla (Acts 18), Phoebe (Rom. 16), and Euodia and Syntyche (Phil. 4), to mention a few. Today many of us are exercised toward deep heart searching in these matters. We hear the cries of those who are hurting and we wonder whether in the past we have been following our traditions more than we have been listening to the Spirit of Christ.

Only eternity will reveal how much God's work was dependent upon faithful women—among them thousands of missionaries around the world—who were called in various capacities to make the gospel known and otherwise serve him.

Judges 4:8–23
The Alloys of Faith

Key thought: *God's work is accomplished by men and women of imperfect faith whose hearts are wholly his.*

Barak was instructed by Deborah to go against Sisera, the Canaanite chief general, and the Lord would deliver him into his hand (vv. 6, 7). While the book of Hebrews records Barak in the list of faith heroes, the account here seems to indicate that though his faith was sincere, it was weak, like the trust of a child who cannot stand alone. Numerous times, therefore, the Holy Spirit emphasized Barak's reluctance to go against Sisera unless Deborah would accompany him (vv. 8–10).

Sooner or later we must learn that God alone is the source of his own image in us. We cannot depend upon the faith of another to do for us what only our own faith can do. The children of Christian parents are especially prone to this danger. Resting in the piety of their parents, they often fail to cultivate their own personal relationship to the Lord. Often, also, a husband will coast along on the spiritual interest and growth of his wife rather than develop his own vital relationship with the Lord Jesus Christ. God's plan calls for each individual to search and find meaningful fellowship in the Lord and then to share and enrich others through that experience.

Jael (vv. 17–22) represents a type which is alloyed with the impurities of guile and treachery. That God may choose to use such an individual cannot be doubted, but the testimony of Scripture is that he uses them in spite of their impurities and not because of them. Jael's burning sympathy for the oppressed Israelites, her faith in Israel's God (whose worship she

Day 16

had espoused in opposition to the idols of Canaan), and her bold execution of her dangerous undertaking all deserve praise, but we do not find her or Ehud enumerated among the examples of faith in Hebrews 11.

Barak's victory over Jabin was the beginning of a series of efforts resulting in the overthrow of the Canaanite kingdom. Little did Barak and Jael know that on that day in the providence of God they were to be the instruments of a decisive victory over the enemy. Who knows what victories God may desire to work today through your life if you are available to him?

Judges 5:1–31
The Song of Deborah

Key thought: *Thank the Lord who always leads us in triumph in Christ over our enemies.* PAUL THE APOSTLE

The victory over Jabin is celebrated in this highly poetical song written by the prophetess Deborah. "For I shall sing" teaches us the wisdom of immediate praise while the heart is full of gratitude; delay dulls heartiness. The same truth is conveyed in the saying, "Eaten bread is soon forgotten."

This beautiful song falls into three sections plus an introduction of praise to the Lord (vv. 1–5) and a concluding contrast between the end of the enemies and lovers of the Lord (v. 31).

In the first stanza (vv. 6–11) the oppression of Israel is described, setting the stage for the leadership of Deborah in delivering the people. No doubt on the human side the great defeat of Jabin was possible because the leaders of Israel "offered themselves so willingly!" (v. 9) and "the people gladly followed" (v. 2). When God's leaders are functioning as they should and the saints of God are willingly cooperating, then the Lord's work has a way of progressing.

The second stanza (vv. 12–18) relates the mustering of Israel's army. It is a story of indifference on the part of some of the tribes (vv. 16, 17—Gilead, Dan, and Asher) and of resolve without action (vv. 15, 16—Reuben). It is also a story of courage, determination, and action on the part of others (vv. 14, 15, 18—Ephraim, Benjamin, Zebulun, Issachar, and Naphtali). Dante said, "The hottest flames in hell are reserved for those who in times of great crisis remain neutral." Certainly we who know truth in Jesus Christ cannot in these days of world crisis remain neutral without someday suffering loss in the presence of Christ.

Finally, the third stanza tells of the battle (vv. 19–23), the heroic act of Jael (vv. 24–27), and the plight of Sisera's mother (vv. 28–30).

The concluding verse emphasizes the triumph of faith and good over evil. It reflects the ultimate triumph of our Lord Jesus Christ over the forces of evil. So we read in the book of Revelation, "You have assumed your great power and have begun to reign. The nations were angry with you, but now it is your turn to be angry with them" (Rev. 11:17, 18). Even so, come, Lord Jesus.

Judges 6:11–24
The Call and Commission of Gideon

Key thought: *Our disappointments are his appointments, to bring us to know him better.*

Gideon's life affords a rich case study of living faith. His life, with its consequent lessons for us, may be viewed in four periods: (1) his call and commission (vv. 11–24); (2) his preparation (vv. 25–40); (3) his victories (7:1—8:21); and (4) his last days (8:22–32).

In the opening scenes of Gideon's record, Israel was once again suffering under oppression due to their sin (vv. 1–10). Gideon had to thresh his grain down inside a stone wine press to avoid detection by Midianite marauders. Suddenly the Lord appeared to Gideon (v. 14) in angelic form as the Angel of the Lord (v. 12) and brought a note of encouragement to him: "The Lord is with you."

Gideon's initial response shows that his mind was occupied with spiritual things even though he was discouraged and probably thought God hadn't heard his prayers. His discouragement is reflected in his, "*If . . . why . . . where . . .*" (v. 13).

If God is with me, will I experience distress and calamity? *Why* have things gone so bad for me, when I have tried to honor him and put him first in my life? Have you ever heard these questions, or perhaps asked them yourself? One answer to this problem is to recognize that God has a larger plan than the one revolving around our life alone or around our immediate circumstances. God's plans are realized not only through the enjoyable experiences of our life but in the bitter as well. God tells us that "*all* things are working together for good," both the sweet and the

Day **17**

bitter, the spices as well as the staples. Although God has revealed to us his general designs, that they are designs of "good," the immediate situations may take on many different hues. From our limited perspective some at present may look unfavorable. Only God himself in his creative love can weave the tapestry.

Imagine a caterpillar puzzled at the strange lines and weavings of a huge tapestry over which it is slowly crawling. One day it becomes a beautiful butterfly. When it gains its strength it flies up over the tapestry. There from the height it sees design in which all the colored threads, light and dark, have their place in the whole.

Then, too, we should not be impatient with God's *timing*. Gideon was. "*Where* are all his wondrous works?" he laments. Having failed to see the goals of his praying realized, he had become discouraged and forlorn. In the Lord's response we have both the solution of Gideon's problem and his divine commission: "Go ... save ... I am sending you" (v. 14). God was about to use his servant in a special manner. Hasn't he said to us, "I will never, never, never, never, never [five times in Greek text] fail you nor forsake you" (Heb. 13:5).

Judges 6:15
Clothe Yourselves with Humility

Key thought: *Humility must be adorned but never "put on."*

Humility, though not highly prized by the world, is one of the chief virtues enjoined upon those who belong to the Lord Jesus Christ. The Savior said, "Therefore anyone who humbles himself as this little child, is the greatest in the Kingdom of Heaven" (Matt. 18:4). Peter wrote, "And all of you serve each other with humble spirits, for God gives special blessings to those who are humble, but sets himself against those who are proud. If you will humble yourselves under the mighty hand of God, in his good time he will lift you up" (1 Pet. 5:5, 6).

Gideon's humility is revealed in his response to the Lord. It is the attitude of surprise reflected in his words, "Sir, how can *I* save Israel? My family is the poorest in the whole tribe of Manasseh, and I am the least thought of in the entire family" (v. 15). D. Martyn Lloyd-Jones in his unexcelled volumes, *Studies in the Sermon on the Mount,* has pointed out what true humility is. Some of these thoughts are shared here.

A truly humble person is not a retiring, weak, nervous individual. In fact, humility is most often noticed in strong personalities: Moses, David, Paul. Further, humility does not consist in glorying in our humbleness by calling attention to ourselves through our dress, voice, or posture. It is not suppression of our personality, or withdrawal as a holy person from the stress of ordinary life into a cloister. Humility, too, should not be confused with being nice. A proud individual may manage to be nice without having any marks of true humility.

What then is humility? It is basically an attitude toward myself and toward others. The attitude toward myself is that of complete self-insufficiency before God. It involves a consciousness that I am nothing in the sight of a holy God. As a sinner before him I must cry out in the words of Charles Wesley: "Just and holy is Thy name/ I am all unrighteousness/ Vile and full of sin I am/ Thou art full and truth and grace." A true sense of one's own unworthiness is found only by looking at Jesus Christ dying in redeeming love for all one's unrighteousness and rebellion. I then exclaim with Isaac Watts: "When I survey the wondrous cross on which the Prince of Glory died/ My richest gain I count but loss and pour contempt on all my pride." Humility, then, begins with a sense of surprise that such a God could come lovingly and mercifully to such a one as I.

Philippians 2:5–8
The Self That He Wills

Key thought: *Some men strive themselves into obscurity; others lose themselves into immortality.*

In our last lesson we found that true humility is an attitude toward self of utter insufficiency in God's sight. Perhaps we should spell this out somewhat more to make it practical.

A truly humble person will feel before God that there is nothing in himself of which he can boast. He will feel no self-reliance or self-assurance in the tasks to which the Lord has called. All reliance on nationality, family relations, color, temperament, knowledge, or talents will be counted as worthless before God. Such a person has self-respect but not self-confidence.

His manner will lack self-assertiveness. He won't push himself on others. Humility doesn't demand anything for itself. A humble person will not claim all his rights or make demands because of his position, privileges, possession, or status. Jesus Christ could have demanded the prerogatives of his deity during his earthly life, but he took on the form of a servant and humbled himself unto death (vv. 5–8).

The humble person will not be self-sensitive. He won't go on the defensive when accused of mistakes or flaws in his thinking, behavior, or performance. He knows he is fallible and capable of all such things even though possibly not actually guilty of the immediate charge. Above all he won't pity himself. As John Bunyan put it, "He that is down need fear no fall."

In his relations to others this humble man will be mild. Others will be able to approach him with perfect ease as they did our Lord Jesus. He will not retaliate evil for evil, but will be patient and longsuffering with others. Finally, he will be docile. He will recognize that he doesn't have all the truth and that others have truth he can learn.

He assesses himself truthfully, neither representing himself to be more nor less in any aspect of his character, achievements, or capabilities.

Humility is not a natural quality but comes from the indwelling Holy Spirit's control of the life (Gal. 5:22–26). Do I want this quality? Then let me (1) meditate on the command to be humble; (2) look to the Lord Jesus as the supreme example; (3) confess my shame, smallness, and imperfection in God's sight; (4) represent my character and abilities honestly; and finally, (5) be done with that selfish self which is the cause of all my trouble and yield myself to Jesus Christ to possess me wholly. Thus will the self that he desires be born.

Judges 6:25–34
The Preparation of Gideon

Key thought: *The quiet preparation of the heart before the Lord readies us for the tumultuous battles of each day.*

Gideon was God's man for Israel's deliverance in this period of history. His success depended not upon his military genius or leadership abilities but upon his relationship to the Lord. Therefore Gideon's spiritual preparation was crucial. It could form a pattern for all who would be available to God for performing his tasks. Gideon was *cleansed* from the paralyzing effect of idolatrous worship (vv. 25–32); *clothed* with the power of the Holy Spirit (vv. 33–35); and *confirmed* in God's will (vv. 36–40). We shall reserve this last point for our next lesson.

(1) Gideon cleansed (vv. 25–32). He was to take his father's seven-year-old bullock (symbolic of the seven years of Midianite oppression) and offer it to the Lord upon the new altar reared up in place of the demolished altar of Baal. This brave act not only showed Gideon's devotion to the Lord, but also served notice to Israel that their God could not tolerate spiritual dilution. God will not share his glory with another.

Interestingly enough, this act of consecration began at home. The sincerity of our abandonment to Christ receives its acid test in our home life. Have we put away the idols of gain, indolence, and pleasure in our personal and family life? If the Christian life doesn't work at home, we might as well forget about impressing the world outside. This young man's faith and consecration apparently influenced even his father's stand for the Lord (v. 31).

(2) Gideon clothed with power (vv. 33–35). The enemy forces were massing for a giant assault upon Israel at Jezreel, an ancient battleground in the Near East. Having put himself at the disposal of the Lord, now that the crisis had arisen, Gideon was invested with the necessary equipment by the Spirit of the Lord. He was "clothed" with the Spirit of God and given the courage and confidence to blow the trumpet that would assemble the forces of Israel to do battle under his leadership (cf. Zech. 4:6; Luke 24:49). God is still looking for warriors with cleansed and consecrated hearts who will by faith claim the power of the Holy Spirit in their daily lives (Eph. 5:18).

Judges 6:35–40
Gideon's Fleece

Key thought: *Divine wisdom is better than signs.*

Gideon still was not completely sure that God was in all this. So he proposed a test. We refer to Gideon's test as "putting out the fleece." Young people are probably more perplexed about how to ascertain the will of God for their lives than about any other single factor. Is this method valid today for finding out God's will?

It must be pointed out at the first that God never promised signs or told us to seek special revelations in determining his will in a decision. We are nowhere encouraged to imitate Gideon. The signs seem to have been given him because of the weakness of his faith and his inability simply to trust the promises that God had already given him.

Further, nowhere are we encouraged to trust in unusual coincidences, circumstances, or our feelings. Satan is apparently able not only to arrange signs, but to bring about remarkable coincidences to tempt us to evil. Our emotions are highly unreliable in most decisions that face us. How then are we to ascertain the will of God in life's decisions?

In one of the finest short treatments of guidance that I have found (*Guidance: Some Biblical Principles,* Inter-Varsity Fellowship), Oliver R. Barclay outlines the only assured method supported by Scripture: "It is, I believe, clear that the New Testament Christians expected to be guided by 'wisdom,' that is, by a sound judgment based on a truly Christian sense of values." This sense of values is formed by constant and penetrating exposure to the Bible. "If you want to know what God wants you to do, ask him and he will

Day 19

gladly tell you" (James 1:5). This is the divine assurance that wisdom is available.

Each decision, then, will be made by seeking prayerfully to judge the matter in the light of the heavenly wisdom (or point of view), applying any specific biblical principles bearing on the matter, and to insure, as far as we know, that we are not being ruled by false motives. Having thus sought his wisdom in the matter we will have to trust him that the decision we have made is right. This procedure is far better and more universally reliable than "putting out the fleece."

Judges 7:1–8
Gideon's Three Hundred

Key thought: *Christ is available to every Christian but not every Christian is available to Christ.*

Midian's armed forces totaled one hundred thirty-five thousand (9:10) compared with Israel's thirty-two thousand (v. 3). Rather poor odds, especially since Israel was not militarily trained or equipped in those days of oppression. But in God's sight the odds were too favorable for Israel! The victory had to be clearly the Lord's doing and not Israel's. Gideon was told to thin out the ranks. So two tests were imposed to eliminate all but the totally committed.

"Send home any of your men who are timid and frightened" (v. 3). Upon this word the cowards turned back. They comprised the bulk of the outfit (two-thirds). Didn't our Lord say that whoever was not willing to deny himself and take up his cross daily could not be his disciple? Paul says, "For his sake we must be ready to face death at every moment of the day." Let cowards flee to other ranks. There is no room for them where Christ's battle is being fought.

But the Lord told Gideon, "There are still too many! Bring them down to the spring and I'll show you which ones shall go with you and which ones shall not" (v. 4). Those who "lapped like dogs" were the three hundred who "drank from their hands" (v. 6). These were chosen and the more indulgent, less watchful, who got down on their knees, were turned back (9,700 men!). Thus, Gideon had his army pared down to 1 percent of its original strength.

One principle that the Lord sets before us in his Word is that he will not share his own glory with another (Isa. 42:8). God will use Gideon and his men but the outcome will be so evidently of God that Gideon will not receive the credit.

Another feature of this strange selection of the army is the lesson that the Lord always seems to move through the dedicated minority among his people. He moves through the few who listen to his words, "If anyone wants to be a follower of mine, let him deny himself and take up his cross and follow me."

Judges 7:9–23
Gideon's Strange Battle

Key thought: *Total commitment is only the first step that leads on to total mobilization and activity.*

Following the mobilization of the small, dedicated army (vv. 1–8) Gideon reconnoitered the Midianite camp and received a wonderful confirmation that God was to be with him in battle (vv. 9–14). The conjunction of events was amazing. Just at the moment that Gideon approached the enemy camp he overheard one Midianite's interpretation of another's dream. It bore a striking similarity to God's promise to Gideon himself (v. 7). The panic which the interpretation implied as existing among the Midianites strengthened Gideon's conviction that God was truly in the whole matter. Contemplating the providence of God, Gideon worshiped (v. 15).

After the briefing (vv. 15–18), the strange battle began (vv. 19–23). Interestingly, even though God had insured victory through a promise, Gideon did not eliminate careful strategy. God's promises do not set aside the need to plan the careful execution of his commands.

Now the moment had arrived. Three hundred men approached the camp of Midian in the middle of the night. Suddenly they broke 300 jars, each containing a burning firebrand, and blew 300 trumpets. The sight and sound, together with the yell, "For the Lord and for Gideon!" (v. 20) confused the Midianites. Possibly they mistook friend for foe in the commotion or they suspected treachery, turned each against the other, and thus were defeated. The peculiar method no doubt was designed to display how completely the victory was of God and not of Israel.

Day 20

In those early morning hours, Gideon and the 300 men learned the unmistakable lesson of unhesitating trust in the veracity and power of their God. It is one thing to be totally committed to Jesus Christ. It is another to be totally mobilized and active in his warfare. Gideon was fearful but nevertheless he moved in obedience and faith.

Judges 8:22–32
The Last Days of Gideon

Key thought: *Teach a child to choose the right path, and even when he is older he will remain upon it.*
PROV. 22:6—HEBREW SENSE

Gideon's last days were not a complement to his previous faithful record. He did some foolish things in his old age that are no doubt recorded as a warning to you and me.

First, while rightly refusing the proferred kingship (vv. 22, 23), he requested the spoil of golden earrings and wrongly made an ephod (v. 27). An ephod was a breastplate inlaid with precious stones and to be used exclusively by the high priests in conversing with God in the tabernacle (Exod. 28:6–30). It seems that because God had communed directly with him, Gideon thought he had the right to preempt this priestly function. With the ephod and the altar (6:26), Israel was "snared" into not going up to the lawful sanctuary of the nation. Thus the way was paved for the people's apostasy to Baal idolatry after Gideon's death (v. 33). For a little folly he sold the people of God into a sinful path.

Second, we are told that he had many wives (v. 30) and a concubine (v. 31). Moses had especially warned the leaders of the nation not to "have too many wives," for they would turn away their hearts from the Lord (Deut. 17:17). Old age has the peculiar temptation of reinstating former inexpediencies as now expedient. Perhaps Gideon's behavior reflected on his early homelife (6:25).

Third, Gideon manifested another weakness in naming his concubine's son Abimelech ("my father is king"—v. 31). Either Gideon himself still secretly aspired to the honor of kingship, even though he had refused to be crowned, or he yielded to the ambitious views of the mother in so naming his son. A peculiar temptation faces many of the Lord's leaders: attempting to share God's glory with him. Such actions God can never bless. He must receive all the credit and glory for what he does or his power ceases to be manifest through us. When we have done all we can, we must take the attitude that in his sight we are unprofitable (useless) servants (Luke 17:10).

Judges 9:1–57
Abimelech:
The Bramble King

Key thought: *Vice is a monster of such hideous mien, that to be hated needs but to be seen. But seen too oft, familiar with her face, we first endure, then pity, then embrace.* ALEXANDER POPE

Chapter 9 is another of those dark records of deceit, murder, and treachery that stain the history of this period under the judges. Though Abimelech was the son of Gideon by his concubine (8:31), he did not follow in the steps of his righteous father. Rather he rebelled and brought great shame to Israel.

Abimelech's first atrocity was to murder the seventy sons of Gideon at Ophrah (v. 5). Only the youngest son, Jotham, escaped death by hiding during the slaughter. Abimelech reflects the ambitious spirit that lusts for power and lets nothing or no one stand in his way. Some feel that Gideon's later years may have influenced Abimelech in his destructive path. Regardless, it is true enough that our children may not stop in the path of sin where we were able to halt. They often follow those little sins we tolerated on out to their disastrous conclusions. The message is too obvious to labor.

Jotham proclaimed in an allegory the irony of Abimelech's dismal plan and ignominious end (vv. 7–21). The "trees" were the Shechemites who came first to Gideon (the "olive tree"—v. 8), then to Gideon's son (the "fig tree"—v. 10), then to another of Gideon's sons (the "grapevine"—v. 12), and finally to Abimelech ("the thorn bush"—v. 14). The irony is found in the types of trees which were able to offer good shade but refused, compared with the low stunted tree. Its

Day 21

drooping, jagged branches and sharp, thick thorns afforded no shade, and scratched those who touched it. It was a fit emblem of the mischievous Abimelech who accepted the kingdom to the ruin of its subjects. His motto was "bow or burn" (v. 15), depicting the truth that "a worthless man soon betrays a tyrant spirit."

Abimelech's folly produced one of the three civil wars in the period (vv. 32–57). His fall and end demonstrate that God was rendering judicial punishment for his wickedness (vv. 56, 57). Let his life be a constant reminder that selfish ambition and vainglory have no place in God's plan for our lives (Phil. 2:3). God "sets himself against those who are proud" (1 Pet. 5:5). Rather, "let him who is greatest among you be servant of all." God's leaders are servant leaders. Requisite to this leadership is a commitment to the selfless promotion of others. In God's program we are all leaders in our own places.

Judges 11:1–29
Jephthah's Victory: Binding the Strong Man

Key thought: *Christianity must defend its claims without being defensive; it must take the offensive without being offensive.*

Jephthah's early beginning was of the most unfavorable sort in comparison with Gideon. He was born out of wedlock (v. 1) and consequently rejected by his half brothers in Gilead's home. Finally he was driven out to lead a sort of vagabond life as a gang leader in the frontier settlement of Tob (vv. 2, 3).

Unfavorable as Jephthah's environment was, however, he was able to rise above it because he knew the Lord personally. There is abroad today a strange attitude that some young people are not responsible for their actions because they come from undesirable neighborhoods or broken homes. It may be true that a bad environment contributes to wrong actions, but we cannot accept the conclusion that any young people are completely unaccountable for their behavior. It is possible to rise above one's environment through the power of the living Christ (1 Tim. 1:15; Phil. 4:13). Through faith in Jesus Christ adverse environment can be a blessing to develop one's instruments and qualify him for the tasks God has for him (Rom. 5:3, 4).

Jephthah tried diplomatic action first against Ammon but to no avail (vv. 12–28). Arms would not be resorted to until all other lawful means of peaceful settlement had failed. Though Jephthah was a "mighty man of valor" (a military hero), he preferred persuasion, on the ground of truth, to force. But when the enemy was massing at the borders there was no other course than to strike at them in their own land before they invaded. (I cannot help comparing this situation with the 1967 invasion of the Sinai under Moshe Dayan.)

Just as the Spirit of the Lord came in power on Jephthah, enabling him to spoil the spoilers (v. 29), so we must not be content as Christians simply to defend our faith. We must make offensive inroads into Satan's kingdom and win men and women from him for Christ, and challenge the powers of darkness, if our own faith and love are not to become cold and stagnant. In our Lord's words we find the same truth, "One cannot rob Satan's kingdom without first binding Satan. Only then can his demons be cast out!" (Matt. 12:29).

Judges 11:30, 31, 34–40
Jephthah's Vow

Key thought: *Our vows ought to be made not to purchase God's favor but to testify to our gratitude.*

Jephthah's vow may have been either an evidence of the deep devotion of his faith in the Lord or (more probably) an evidence of his lack of trust in the assurance given to him through the Holy Spirit (v. 29). We would do better to trust God's Word and the inward assurance of the Holy Spirit than to bargain with God by promising some great sacrifice in order to procure his favor. We also should avoid rash vows whose consequences we may afterward regret. Every vow should be fulfilled unless by so doing we sin more against God and the welfare of our neighbor than if we do not fulfill it (cf. Saul—1 Sam. 14).

As to how Jephthah fulfilled his vow there are two main conclusions. The one holds that he offered his daughter as a human sacrifice. A chief argument usually advanced is the fact that during the period of the judges spiritual conditions were corrupt and standards low.

The other view seems much more credible and harmonious with all the facts. Jephthah was well acquainted with the Mosaic law, as his letter to Ammon reflects (vv. 16–22). He would therefore be aware that such sacrifice was an abomination before the Lord (Lev. 18:21; 20:2–5). But all the conditions are fulfilled if we conclude that he devoted his only daughter to lifelong virginity (a spiritual burnt offering consecrated to the Lord).

It should be noted that (1) she went to bemoan her "fate" (v. 38), not her life; (2) Jephthah is said to have performed his vow and immediately it is added "so she was never married" (v. 39), which would be superfluous if her death were meant; and (3) Israel would never have perpetuated a celebration of human sacrifice which was contrary to the law (v. 40). What they did go yearly to "praise" was her willingness to obey her father and sacrifice her own natural ambitions as the conqueror's daughter for self-renouncing godliness.

Judges 12:1–6
Jephthah's Vengeance

Key thought: *One may criticize another player only if one is playing the game successfully himself.*

Following the defeat of Ammon under Jephthah, the tribe of Ephraim once again flamed a civil war against their brother tribe, the Gileadites. Once the battle with Ammon was over and Israel had come off victorious, Ephraim approached Jephthah and asked why they had not been included in the warfare (v. 1). Their quarrelsome spirit, no doubt due to their own lusterless activities, revealed a deep-seated sin of envy.

Once again Jephthah diplomatically sought to avert a conflict by explaining the facts which led to his just exclusion of the Ephraimites from helping (vv. 2, 3). But conflict was unavoidable (v. 4).

Ironically, it was the Ephraimites' tongue that accused the Gileadites of being "outcasts" (v. 4). Now it was they who were the fugitives, and their tongue was the instrument of their destruction. They could not pronounce "Shibboleth" (v. 6). So God's retributive judgments appear in this present world, displaying the truth that he is the moral Governor, even though the forces of the evil one may temporarily reign.

Another lesson for us emerges from this account. Ephraim's spirit seems to be found today in some Christians who are willing to let others confront non-Christians with the gospel, but reserve the right from the sidelines to criticize and even condemn their brothers and sisters for the way they have gone into the battle.

Christian involvement may be illustrated by three aspects of a football game. There are those, first of all, who are not involved with football at all. They are out of the stadium and don't even know that a game is in progress. Another group, like Ephraim, are on the sidelines rooting and booing while they eat their snacks and sip their sodas. Others are in the game. They are producing the action, executing the strategy, and winning the conflicts. To which group do you belong?

Judges 13:1–25
The Birth of Samson

Key thought: *Samson's life is a great opportunity and a disastrous failure.* G. CAMPBELL MORGAN

Samson's life is a fascinating character study rich in spiritual instruction. It begins with the story of a faithful mother and father. There are three focal points in this unparalleled account of the birth of a judge.

First, the Holy Spirit through a threefold emphasis stressed the "Nazirite character of the child who was to be born" (vv. 4, 5, 7, 14). Both mother and child were to abstain from any product of the vine. Samson was to allow his hair to grow in accordance with the Mosaic law for the dedication vow of a Nazirite (Num. 6:1ff.). Apparently the Nazirite consecration was to begin with Samson's mother and be uniquely effective in the son's life from his birth (v. 5) until his death (v. 7).

Second, the godly and humble response of the parents of Samson is highlighted in these verses. The barrenness of Manoah's wife apparently served to prepare her and her husband for this great experience. They showed a sensitivity to God's movements born out of prayer and an equal sensitivity to each other's feelings, cultivated through fellowship and communion.

Third, in this account we see something about the "Angel of the Lord" (vv. 3, 9, 15–23). In verse 22 Manoah finally realized that the Angel of the Lord was in reality God himself in angelic-human appearance. Many would identify these as Christophanies or preincarnate manifestations of Christ. His name is given as "secret" (better translated "wonderful"—v. 18), the same title of the Messiah in Isaiah 9:6.

Day **23**

They called the child's name Samson (v. 24), derived either from *shamesh,* the sun (as a shining light to deliver Israel), or from *shemesh,* to minister (as a consecrated Nazirite).

Judges 14:1–20
Samson at Timnah

Key thought: *Don't be teamed with those who do not love the Lord, for what do the people of God have in common with the people of sin?* PAUL THE APOSTLE

The secret of Samson's life lies in his yieldedness to the "Spirit of the Lord [who] began to excite him" (13:25). The word translated "excite" is closely related to the blacksmith's anvil. The smith would repeatedly strike the implement on the anvil. Later in the usage of the word the thought conveyed was more the idea of "thrust" or "impel." So the Spirit drove him out into exploits for the Lord (cf. Mark 1:12). The first recorded venture was at Timnah where he married a Philistine woman.

Samson's desire for a Philistine wife, though it grieved his God-fearing parents (v. 3), and was probably partly to gratify his own fleshly desire, apparently arose from the Lord (v. 4). Samson, unlike the previous judges, didn't seek to lead an army but to be an army in himself!

The account of Samson's unusual slaying of the lion barehanded and his return some time later to find honey in the carcass is set in the context of oriental marriage custom. After the arrangement by the parents (vv. 1–4), the bride and groom remained betrothed until the feast time (v. 10). Finding the honey in the lion provided the occasion to fashion a difficult riddle that would provide a point of frustration and provocation for the Philistines and thus allow Samson a justification to battle with them.

All would have worked well had it not been for Samson's Achilles' heel. Betrayed by his new wife's incessant weeping (crocodile tears!), he was forced to provide thirty new suits for the wedding fellows. So, in the sudden power of the Holy Spirit granted to him (v. 19), he went to battle against one of the Philistines' Pentapolis cities, Ashkelon.

What might have been a great victory for the Nazirite developed into an insignificant skirmish because Samson had made an unwise choice in his future bride. In his zeal, he forgot to take time to choose a woman prayerfully and carefully, one who would not only satisfy his carnal desires, but be a helper suited to his spiritual needs.

Judges 15:1–8
Foxes and Firebrands

Key thought: *It is better to be alienated from the world, if need be, than to be in love with it, be ensnared by it, and perish with it.*

Again Samson sought an occasion to fight against Israel's enemies, the Philistines. He purposely chose the time of wheat harvest to return to the Philistine city of Timnah where he had a short time ago angrily left his wife who had betrayed him. Perhaps he strongly suspected that her father would have given her to someone else to get revenge on him for killing thirty Philistine soldiers at Ashkelon (14:19).

When Samson learned from his father-in-law's lips that indeed his wife had been given to another (v. 2), he had the necessary reason to justify his military exploits against them. Finding a pack or two of jackals (foxes usually travel alone), he connected 150 pairs together at the tails by means of torches (firebrands) which he set on fire. Then he turned flaming jackals into the luscious grain fields and vineyards.

When the Philistines learned that Samson had destroyed the crops because of the injustice done to him by his wife's father, they sought vengeance upon the father and burned (the home of both him and the daughter (v. 6). That evil which she and her father had sought to escape by betraying Samson to the Philistine lords (14:15), they brought on themselves.

But Samson was not appeased by this cruelty. Further enraged against the Philistines, he said, "Now my vengeance will strike again!" (v. 7). So he went out against them and won a great victory. Their losses were great. He smote them "with great fury" means

Day **24**

literally with "hip and thigh" (v. 8) which is difficult to understand. It probably means a cruel slaughter.

Samson was learning by bitter experience the wisdom of his parents' advice concerning his lifetime partner (cf. 14:3). In spite of his mistakes, however, his actions reveal a deep sense of right and a desire to deliver Israel from her enemies. God was able to use Samson to effect his own will.

Judges 15:9–20
A Thousand with a Jawbone

Key thought: *Ours is no day to concede victory to the enemies of Christianity but to move out as never before to claim all men for Christ.*

Angered and filled with the spirit of revenge, the Philistines came to Lehi in Judah to rout Samson. Here a pathetic thing happened. Instead of arising to defend the noble Samson from their common enemy, the men of Judah bargained to deliver up their deliverer to save their own skin. They admitted their defeated condition: "Don't you realize that the Philistines are our rulers?" (v. 11).

Samson was much nobler, for he willingly, notwithstanding his great strength, submitted himself to be bound and delivered to the Philistines to protect his people. When confronted with the enemy, the "strength of the Lord came upon Samson" (v. 14) and the exercise of his great strength caused the ropes to burn up, perhaps from the friction. Then he seized a jawbone of an ass and with it he fought off and killed a thousand Philistine soldiers. Under the Spirit of God

Samson was an army in himself. His single-handed victory was a divine rebuke to his cowardly brethren in Judah.

Paul says, "We are not fighting against people made of flesh and blood, but against ... great evil princes of darkness who rule this world; and against huge numbers of wicked spirits in the spirit world" (Eph. 6:12).

Some believers, as the men of Judah in our story, have conceded victory to the forces of ungodliness in our day. But here and there the Spirit of God is still at work in a few Samsons who are going into enemy territory with the armor of God "to knock down the devil's strongholds" (2 Cor. 10:4). They are not defeated but believe that his territory can be successfully invaded and claimed for Christ in our day.

Judges 16:4–20
Samson and Delilah

Key thought: *Samson, when strong and brave, strangled a lion; but he could not strangle his own lust. He burst the fetters of his foes, but not the cords of his own passions.* AMBROSE

The story of Samson and Delilah is well known. The lessons it teaches are not so well known. In this chapter of Samson's life we see him becoming a slave to lust. Temptation cannot be trifled with, without being caught in its snare.

What was at first a leading of God to invade the Philistine strongholds (14:1ff.) he now degenerated into a capricious gratification of his own desires. Still conscious of his Nazirite consecration (v. 17), he nevertheless flattered himself that he could toy with this temptress, Delilah.

Three times Samson allowed himself to be exposed to needless temptation. Each time he was drawn closer to the fatal trap. In the third round he even permitted the seven locks of his Nazirite hair to be woven and fastened to the weaver's loom (vv. 13, 14). Those who walk on the edge of a precipice are inviting a disastrous fall.

Delilah was a woman who was willing to sell not only her body but also her character for a tenuous promise of silver from the Philistine lords. "Like a serpent, she coiled closer and closer round her victim each time; and he, with amazing infatuation, as a bird fascinated with the eye of the destroyer, ventured nearer and nearer the temptation" (Fausset). "Delilah" means the "languishing" or "pining" one, perhaps indicating the dilution of her personality that resulted from multiple liaisons. Contrast this true picture with the Playboy counterpart.

Samson confessed that his strength lay in his Nazirite vow of consecration "to God" (v. 17), of which his uncut hair was a symbol (cf. Num. 6:5). The secret of his great strength lay in his "set-apartness" for the Lord. When his hair was cut, the writer notes that "the Lord had left him" (v. 20). And the tragedy of it all was that Samson didn't realize it.

Judges 16:21–31
Samson's Death

Key thought: *Ask for this great deliverer now, and find him, eyeless at Gaza, at the mill with slaves.* MILTON

Samson's obituary describes his pitiful last days, blinded, grinding (a woman's job) with the slaves at the mill (v. 21). Once a mighty warrior whom no Philistine would dare to mock, now a prisoner providing entertainment and laughter for his captors.

Irony runs through the account. He whom no man could bind was bound by a woman. His eyes had been the avenue through which he had first been bound by his lust; his eyes were now destroyed. He who could capture a city single-handed could not subdue his own spirit (cf. Prov. 16:32). Gaza, once the scene of his sin (16:1–3) and valiance, was now the scene of his chastisement and slavery.

No doubt the significance of Samson's spectacular end is to be found in the reference to the Philistines' god Dagon (vv. 23, 24). Combining the body of a fish and a man's head under the fish's head, and a woman's feet joined to its tail, Dagon was thus found in Sennacherib's palace at Nineveh. Our mermaid is the modern relic. A great assembly of people, gathered to sacrifice (probably human victims) to Dagon, provided the occasion to praise the heathen fish god for their victory over the Jew, Samson, a worshiper of Jehovah. God was to show that he, not Dagon, delivered up Samson for his sin.

Requesting a rest, Samson grasped the main pillars of the temple. Once more finding favor with the Lord by confession, he pushed with all his strength. The structure collapsed, destroying the Philistine lords and 3,000 men and women (v. 27).

Though it may be true that "those he killed at the moment of his death were more than those he had killed during his entire lifetime" (v. 30), he nevertheless died in subjection to the heathen. Were it not for this final pardoning grace of the Lord he would have died with little permanent gain to his credit. Israel still remained in servitude to Philistine oppression after twenty years (v. 31).

Proverbs 6:26, 27; 16:32
Samson's Epitaph

Key thought: *As the beauty of a rose lies not only in its outward appearance but also in its inward fragrance, so the Christian's beauty lies in his or her genuineness.*

Samson's life is the story of a great opportunity and a disastrous failure. We must mark its lessons permanently upon our hearts.

Unlike Jephthah, Samson was born into a godly home of praying parents. What a great advantage spiritually and morally a Christ-centered home can be for a young person. It can create and inculcate a sense of values and a quality of life that will be indelibly imprinted upon the entire future life (Prov. 22:6). Such a home will provide the channel for the indispensable truth of eternal salvation through personal trust in Jesus Christ, the Savior (2 Tim. 3:15). Here a child will also find genuine love wed to discipline (the investment of duty) in such a manner that it produces a responsible, useful individual (Prov. 13:24). All this Samson had from his birth.

Further, this mighty man was consecrated to God from birth by the Nazirite vow. We cannot help but compare Samson with John the Baptist who was likewise a Nazirite from birth (Luke 1:15). How similar their beginnings; how different their ends. The curtain on Samson's final scene came down on his death as a prisoner because of his uncontrolled lusts. His epitaph: "He could not control his own spirit." John's final scene closed with him a prisoner for Jesus Christ. His epitaph: "Among those born of women, there has not been a greater than John." The former's life was marked with many exploits of outward strength and few of moral strength; the latter's life with no recorded act of physical strength but many evidences of moral power.

Our service for God can be profitless and destroyed if not joined with moral and spiritual strength. We must find the Holy Spirit not only the source of our power for service but also the source of our inner motivations (Gal. 5:22, 23). What we are inwardly becoming will ultimately shape the value of all our hands touch. Samson's failure can largely be traced to lack of self-control over his passions (cf. Gal. 5:23).

Judges 17:1–13
Micah's Idol

Key thought: *And then, instead of worshiping the glorious, ever-living God, they took wood and stone and made idols for themselves . . . Instead of believing what they knew was the truth about God, they deliberately chose to believe lies.* ROM. 1:23, 25

In the last five chapters of Judges (17–21) we find case studies of corrupted lives. Chronologically the events probably occurred between the death of Joshua and the rule of first judge.

Depicted are the period's spiritual chaos in its gross idolatry (chs. 17, 18), the period's moral chaos in its debased perversion (ch. 19), and the period's civil chaos in its anarchy (chs. 20, 21). These chapters cast further light on the consequences of departure from God. The case studies are like an X-ray picture of the heart of a generation who "did not worship Jehovah as their God" (2:10).

Also, if these events transpired in the interval between Joshua's death and the first judge, they reveal the short time it takes for the heart to grow cold toward God and leave him unless it is constantly renewed (cf. Gal. 1:6—so soon, quickly).

In chapter 17 we get a glimpse of the typical way idolatry began in an Israelite home. A son, named Micah, stole a large amount of money from his mother, who pronounced a curse upon the thief. When Micah confessed, instead of punishing him for the theft, she took part of the money and bought a graven image to place in her home. Micah appointed one of his own sons to serve as a priest until a Levite was hired (vv. 7–13). Thus, an idolatrous shrine was established under the deceit of the worship of the Lord (v. 13).

Perhaps the greatest lesson from this sad account is a warning about the folly of setting up man-made religions or practices that are no way countenanced by the revealed truth of God in the Bible. Jesus condemned this error in the Pharisees: "You are simply rejecting God's laws and trampling them under your feet for the sake of your traditions" (Mark 7:9). Let us be sure that whatever we believe and practice finds its source in the Bible.

Judges 18:1–31
The Road to National Idolatry

Key thought: *A fool and his gods are soon parted.*

Apostasy from God soon spreads its venom from family to family until a whole community is infected and then a nation. In this lesson we can see some of the fruits of a self-styled religion. The story involves the accidental discovery of Micah's idolatrous shrine by the tribal scouts of the Danites. Feeling that God would bless them more if they had this shrine in their new country, the Danites bribed Micah's priest to go with them and then stole the graven image.

We should see from Micah's experience that when a shrine (or religion) is built out of straw and fodder, it first of all provides an inadequate shelter from the "storm." Second, it quickly falls when assailed, leaving the owner empty and destitute. Micah had replaced (1) God's house at Shiloh (v. 31) with his own sanctuary; (2) God's divine method of revelation through his Word and prophets with his own ephod and teraphim; and (3) God's ordinances with his own self-consecrated priesthood. His spiritual poverty is seen in his lament to the Danite bandits: "You've taken away all my gods and my priest, and I have nothing left!" (v. 24).

If our idols consist of money, position, and power, it doesn't matter what religious banner we live under. Our life will be empty of spiritual reality before God. And when our gods fall, we exclaim, "What do I have left?"

Jesus said, "For God is Spirit, and we must have his help to worship as we should" (John 4:23). Sincerity in religious matters isn't enough. God must be worshiped in the truth of his self-revelation found in the Bible

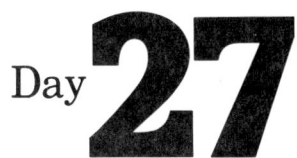

Day 27

and found supremely in his Son, Jesus Christ
(Heb. 1:1, 2). Let us never be guilty of substituting
religion and gods of human invention for the reality of
the true God (1 John 5:20, 21).

Judges 19:1–30; Romans 1:21–25
Moral Chaos

Key thought: *A people never rises higher morally than their religion, however lower they fall than their profession.* FAUSSET

A little known fact about the coherence of society comes to light in this chapter. There is an unmistakable connection between decadence in the knowledge of the true God and the breakdown in morality of the family and society. One needs only turn to Paul's description in Romans 1:18–32 to verify this biblical teaching. Departure from God leads to various forms of self-styled religion or to atheism, which in turn can erode every reason for maintaining a Christian morality.

This chapter reveals several types of moral decadence. A Levite, who because of his priestly service was supposed to set an example among the people, took a secondary wife, called a concubine, who got angry with him and ran away. Further on in the account are evidences of even more serious moral sickness seen in the sexual perversion of the men of Gibeah (v. 22) and in their criminal abuse of the Levite's concubine (vv. 25, 26). So fierce was the husband's indignation that it prompted him to violate all natural repugnance for the mutilation of his concubine's corpse in order to arouse all Israel to vengeance (vv. 27–30). That such moral evil could be performed outside Israel in a pagan society no one would deny, but how tragic when found within the borders of a land thoroughly bathed in biblical morality. In a nation as conscious as ours is of imminent daily violence, someone needs to rise up and call us back to the God of our fathers before moral chaos breaks out unbridled upon us and our children. We should be reminded once again that this moral degeneracy took place among a generation of young people "who did not worship Jehovah as their God" (Judges 2:10).

Judges 17:6;
18:1, 7; 19:1; 21:25
The New Morality

Key thought: *If the foundations have been torn down, what can the righteous do but flee?* PSA. 11:3

You will notice in each of the five passages cited for this study the accounts of the prevalence of evil are connected with the absence of civil government or governor. It is no accident that Christianity teaches that civil authority is appointed by God to impose restraint upon the natural evil tendencies of man (cf. Rom. 13:1ff.).

Consider the current manifestation of lawlessness known as the "new morality." In this teaching, no moral norms of right and wrong guide the Christian's behavior, other than the demand that the "spirit of love" be expressed on every occasion. The particular situation determines what is right or wrong. Not even premarital sex (we are told) can be labelled as wrong in itself. Thus the end justifies the means—under the guise of an "updated" and "come-of-age" Christian religion. Today, as in the days of the judges, the absence of authority and law results in "every man doing that which is right in his own eyes."

In my opinion we are witnessing the fruit of a former generation of ethical preaching from our pulpits without a concurrent strong doctrinal emphasis. The theology of Christ and the apostles was played down by false prophets, as if in conflict with Christian ethical teachings. As a result many tried to maintain and teach a morality that had no explicit basis in the reality of Christ and his redemption. One poet wrote: "When nations are to perish in their sins / 'Tis in the church the leprosy begins."

Day 28

Love is blind without the eyes of God's laws. The "new morality" is proving disastrous for the love of many well-meaning people. Recently in *Chicago Today,* columnist Harriet Van Horne lamented the evil side effects of the new morality. Describing how in the mid-sixties she was firmly on the side of the sexual revolution, she now has revised her opinion and points out the evident dehumanizing and socially corrupting effects of the sex mania.

> The new morality, which decrees that every red-blooded mortal under 80 aggrandize his desires to the maximum and satisfy them to the ultimate, is actually immoral in the most primal sense; immoral because it violates the principles that hold society together. Among them: respect for the functions of the human body, respect for the integrity of the family, and the innocence of the young.
>
> The Roman banquets featured orgies that would stagger the glorious liberation. There is no evidence that such depravity contributed to the grandeur that was Rome. Indeed, such events are always described in the chapters setting forth the reasons for the fall of Rome.

If one advocates a revolution of authentic sexuality, then let that voice be heard. But what Christian can endorse a sexual revolution that ultimately dehumanizes man and woman?

Matthew 15:18–20;
Romans 1:32; 2:12–15
What Behavior Is Right?

Key thought: *Right and wrong are not matters of human opinion any more than the multiplication table.*
C. S. LEWIS

Population growth and increased urbanization have generated a mobile, impersonal, anonymous life style that makes enforcement of moral codes difficult. Secularization has resulted in the sense of the "death of God" and has given rise to a nonjudgmental view of human behavior, free of praise or censure. As Jim Casey said in *Grapes of Wrath,* "There ain't no sin and there ain't no virtue. There's just stuff people do."

When we say that certain types of human behavior such as selfishness or adultery are wrong and other behavior such as kindness or integrity are right, we are affirming that persons possess a moral sentiment. To say that this idea of a moral sense is unsound, because different cultures and different ages have had quite different moralities, is a cop-out. The fact is they all evidence moral awareness.

Now if it be granted that all human beings everywhere have a certain sense of right and wrong, then it must also be observed that no one keeps his own moral law. Either yesterday or today we failed to do unto others as we would have had them do unto us. We were unfair to our children because we were so tired, angry with our wife because she was unreasonable, etc. We have all sorts of excuses for not doing what we know we should.

If we will concede that such a moral sentiment exists, and that most people do not keep it, then we must admit that the source of such a sentiment is really not in human instincts or drives. Something separate from these enables us to know which of these drives we "ought" to follow, even though we in fact do not, or do not even want to, follow them. This something is in reality a revelation, being pressed upon us from above and beyond, that wants us to behave in a certain way that we call right in contrast with the opposite behavior called wrong.

The Christian knows that this moral sentiment is in reality the influence of the eternal God trying to get us to recognize our sinfulness (cf. Rom. 2:14–16). This same God is revealed in Jesus Christ, who forgives men their wrong behavior and provides the power to do what is right and good in his sight (Rom. 6:17, 18, 22).

Judges 20:1–48
Civil Chaos

Key thought: *Pride goes before destruction and haughtiness before a fall.* PROV. 16:18

Departure from God and absence of leadership produce chaos in a nation. Here we find civil war breaking out between the unrepentant Benjamite tribe and the other eleven tribes of Israel, who were justly indignant over the wrong committed by Benjamin in regard to the death of the Levite's concubine (cf. 20:6).

When Benjamin was confronted with the wrong that some of their people at Gibeah had committed, they chose to defend their unrighteous cause and to go to war with the rest of the nation rather than deliver up the guilty men.

The war that followed (20:19–48) brought heavy and needless losses on both sides. Eventually, the eleven tribes, who outnumbered Benjamin nearly twenty to one, won a complete victory. So destructive was the war for Benjamin that only a handful of its original 26,000 soldiers survived.

At least two lessons emerge from this incident. On the one hand, in the righteous indignation of the nation against the wrongdoers at Gibeah, we find an example of a right spirit toward injustice and unpunished evil. Indifference to evil, easy connivance at its commission, and the absence of zealous care to clear one's self from complicity in it, are marks of declension in religion. The opposite spirit characterizes soundness in faith (cf. 2 Cor. 7:11).

On the other hand, this chapter contains a warning for us about the consequences of harboring evil in our individual lives or in the life of a nation. The Gibeahites through pride screened the guilty from

punishment and made themselves responsible for their crime. So a Christian is called not only to put away evil from his life but to "reprove" the unfruitful works of darkness (Eph. 5:11).

For Jesus on one occasion it meant driving men and animals from the temple which had been profaned by business activities (John 2). On another it meant verbally denouncing the injustices and hypocrisies of the Pharisees (Matt. 23). What the "reproving" work will involve for us must be individually and prayerfully considered. But it will certainly at times be included in our activities as those who follow the Lord Jesus Christ.

Romans 13:1–7; 1 Peter 2:13–17
Civil Rights and Civil Disobedience

Key thought: *Law and order are inseparable—think about that!*

We live in an era of sensitive consciences and civil disobedience. Many in our day are troubled with agonizing conflicts between their consciences and civil law. Whatever else others may advocate, Christians must be obedient to the admonitions in God's Word about civil government.

In the first place the Christian is instructed that the authority of civil government is divinely ordered (Rom. 13:1). Officers of the government authority, therefore, are to be respected and obeyed in their official capacities as "servants of God" to promote good and punish evil (Rom. 13:4–14). Government has a sphere of appointed authority over us and as such exacts certain rightful demands such as taxes and respect (Rom. 13:6, 7; Luke 20:25).

If we reject the authority in the civil magistrate we are rejecting something God has ordered (Rom. 13:2). Christians who break the constituted law at will are not only in danger of flouting the divine authority but are wounding themselves inwardly by violating their conscience toward God's will (Rom. 13:5). Further, one should expect and accept wrath from the government if he finds he must violate a certain law to call attention to or test its injustice (Rom. 13:4).

As Christians we are generally to submit to every civil institution (1 Pet. 2:13, 14). When the law seems to work evil rather than good, we are to call attention to the injustice by every lawful means in order to bring about a change of the law. Nowhere are we given any sanction to break the law simply because it seems to us to be unjust. If we break laws at will, by the same principle we give others grounds to break laws that we believe are good but with which they do not agree.

The only apparent specific exceptions to the above principles that are found in the Bible relate to civil government's command to murder children, and forbidding the worship of God or the preaching of the gospel (cf. Exod. 1:15–17; Dan. 3:13ff.; Acts 4:19, 20). In such cases civil authority has stepped out of its rightful sphere into God's sphere and has ordered actions that are contrary to the commands of God.

For some sincere Christians, killing in war is just such a case of the government's commanding something contrary to Jesus' teachings and they rightfully refuse to participate in military service. In our country this does not constitute a violation of civil law, but is provided for under the provisions for conscientious objection in our laws. For other Christians, participation in the military does not seem to constitute a violation of God's commands, and they will support their government in war. Young men desperately need help in these areas of painful decisions and the church should seek to provide as much understanding, guidance, and help as it can.

Judges 21:1–25
Healing the Scars

Key thought: *Disobedience spins a web of sticky problems.*

The final episode in the case studies of conditions during the period of the Judges involves the healing of a wound inflicted in the civil war between the Benjamites and the rest of Israel. War is bad enough in itself, but when zeal for a righteous cause leads to unnecessary devastations, more harm arises than is justifiable. The divine cause always takes into account the human cause.

So unrelenting was the vengeance of the Israelites against the unrepentant Benjamites that out of the original 26,000 men (20:15), only a fraction remained alive (20:39). This unnecessary slaughter threatened extinction of the small Benjamite tribe. Further, to add insult to injury, the Israelites by a rash oath prohibited marriage of their daughters to the surviving men of Benjamin (21:1). It would have been better to break such an unwise oath than belligerently to hold to it at the cruel expense of their brothers. To complicate matters further, the Israelites cruelly attacked the inhabitants of Jabesh-Gilead and killed all the inhabitants except 400 virgin girls (21:8–12).

And if this were not enough, they devised a scheme of abducting the remaining 200 women needed, from the yearly festival at Bethel (21:16–24).

Two thoughts emerge from these incidents. First of all, we should recognize that it is possible to champion God's cause in a wrong manner. Our zeal may not be tempered with sound Christian principles or our motives controlled by the love of Christ. In such a case, our work will produce no permanent testimony for

Day 30

God's glory. Jehu in the Old Testament (2 Kings 9, 10; Hosea 1:4) and the disciples in the New (Luke 9:51–56) illustrate this principle.

We can also clearly see in this chapter how one sin leads to other sins and further complications, until a web is spun that ensnares practically every area of one's life. The remedy? Confess your sins (1 John 1:9) daily and by God's grace forsake those things. Start each day with a clean slate no matter what the personal cost.

John 16:21–24
Power or Defeat?

Key thought: *God at the center of life fills it with power; self at the center of life fills it with defeat.*

As we look back over the history of the period of time from Joshua through the Judges, certain truths stand out.

In Joshua, we discovered that victory is possible. Faith in God's promises actually does bring God's power and provisions to one's life, just as surely as it brought to Israel the possession of the promised land. Remember the key verse of Joshua: "So Joshua took the entire land just as the Lord had instructed Moses: and he gave it to the people of Israel as their inheritance.... So the land finally rested from its war" (Josh. 11:23). The Christian can claim as did Paul: "I can do everything God asks me to [meet every circumstance and battle of life] with the help of Christ who gives me the strength and power" (Phil. 4:13), and "I have fought long and hard for my Lord, and through it all I have kept true to him" (2 Tim. 4:7).

Let us keep constantly before us the truth of Judges 2: "They abandoned Jehovah. . . . So the anger of the Lord flamed out. . . . He left them to the mercy of their enemies . . . [and] the people were in this terrible plight" (vv. 12, 14, 15). Departure from a living relationship with Jesus Christ will spell defeat and disaster in the life of a Christian (Heb. 3:12–14).

Defeat in the life of a Christian arises from two basic disorders, the first giving rise to the second. Our first danger lies in abandoning the nuptial love of our hearts toward Christ and toward other Christians (Rev. 2:4). Faith is the fuel that operates our hearts. It is faith in God and God's Word that enables us to open our lives, receive Christ's love, and respond with love to him and to others. When belief causes our love to cool, we face the second danger. We become slaves to disobedience as did the Israelites in the times of the judges (Judges 3:7ff.). So faithlessness begets unfaithfulness in love and in turn leads to disobedience.

On the other hand, victory and power for the Christian pivot also upon these two points. Do I abide continually in the love of Christ (John 15:4, 9, 10; Jude 20, 21)? Then, is my love for Christ proved by obedience to the Lord's commands and in my relationship to others (John 14:23; 15:10)? This is the secret of the life of power and fulfillment and it delivers us from defeat and emptiness.

SOME FINAL THOUGHTS

A closing word from one of the "greats" in our age, Dr. Abraham Kuyper (pastor, theologian, statesman, philosopher, and scientist), reflects my sentiments about the pages of this small book:

> Contemplative thought, reflections and meditations on the soul's nearness unto God ... tend to draw the soul away from the abstract in doctrine and life, back to the reality of religion ... [and] lead the soul back to the living Fountain itself, from whence these waters flow.
>
> Stress on creedal confession, without drinking of these waters, runs dry in barren orthodoxy, just as truly as spiritual emotion, without clearness in confessional standards, makes one sink in the bog of sickly mysticism.
>
> Only he who feels, perceives and knows that he stands in personal fellowship with the living God, and who continually tests his spiritual experience by the Word, is safe. He exhibits strength, and maintains, for his part, the power of religion in his home, among his associates and in the world at large, and inspires with reverence even those who are despisers of God and his word.
>
> My prayer is, that the Meditations here offered may establish, advance, or restore, such a healthy state of soul with many a child of God.
>
> To have reached this end in the case of even one heart would furnish abundant reason for praise and thanksgiving (*Near to God,* p. 6).